BROR BLIXEN: THE AFRICA LETTERS

BROR BLIXEN

THE

AFRICA

LETTERS

TRANSLATED AND INTRODUCED BY
G. F. V. KLEEN

ST. MARTIN'S PRESS • NEW YORK

Design by Jessica Shatan

Library of Congress Cataloging-in-Publication Data

Blixen-Finecke, Bror, baron von, 1886–1946.
    The Africa letters/Bror Blixen: edited and with an introduction
by Romolus Kleen.
        p.   cm.
    Translated from the Swedish by R. Kleen.
    ISBN 0-312-01468-6: $18.95
    1. Blixen-Finecke, Bror, baron von, 1886–1946.   2. Hunters—Kenya—
Correspondence.   3. Husbands—Kenya—Correspondence.   4. Kenya—
Social life and customs.   I. Kleen, Romolus. II. Title.
SK17.B55A3 1988
967.6—dc19   87-28402
                                                                CIP

First Edition
10   9   8   7   6   5   4   3   2   1

CONTENTS

ACKNOWLEDGMENTS

I wish to record my thanks to the following people for their assistance in the production of this edition of Blix's book:

Gosta Adelsward for allowing me to use his letter in my introduction; Ulf Aschan for the many pleasant hours we have spent together talking about *Waboga;* the late John Belcher for all the work he did, and the interest he took, on my behalf with such good humor; Jens Borg for providing a photograph of Kuhnert's picture; Hans von Blixen-Finecke for lending me his photograph album, and for the discussions we had about this shared uncle when we crossed the Sahara together; Polly Drysdale for her many letters to me on the subject of Blix; Hedvig Ersman for having tidied up my rather amateurish maps; Jacqueline "Cockie" Hoogterp for all the joyous memories we shared from the days I lived with her and Blix at Babati; Elspeth Huxley for letting me use her photographs; Malin Kleen—my beloved wife—for simply existing, and for putting up with my, at times, bad temper during the progress of this translation of Blix's book; Kathy Moore for all her typing, and for her almost unbelievable ability to decipher my handwriting, which I can hardly do myself; and most of all, Mary S. Lovell for all her extremely intelligent, encouraging, friendly, and very professional advice, without which this edition would never have been accomplished.

INTRODUCTION

To the millions of cinema-goers who saw the film *Out of Africa*, Bror Blixen may be known only as the husband of Karen Blixen, who wrote under the name Isak Dinesen. In that film, based both on his wife's book *Out of Africa* and on the Judith Thurman biography of Dinesen, *Isak Dinesen: The Life of a Storyteller*, Bror was portrayed as a playboy, charming and adventurous but also hopelessly irresponsible. In earlier biographies of Karen—though not in Karen's own writings—he was painted even more harshly, not just as an irresponsible husband but as a coarse and lecherous philanderer.

In fact, Bror and Karen Blixen's lives came together for little more than a decade. The couple courted in 1912 and 1913 and were married in 1914. Seven years later, in 1921, they separated. They were divorced in the early twenties. Despite the fact that both went on to live rich and interesting lives, they did not ever again spend much time together; Karen left Africa for good in 1931.

Of course, Bror Blixen did have darker facets to his character, as most of us do. Even if he did not, there would still be the fact that Bror and Karen were very different people, with very different interests and passions, and therefore any portrait of him painted by those primarily interested in examining his ability to fulfill the needs of a certain other person would likely reveal him as lacking in important qualities. But most of those who knew Bror well recall him as sunny, likeable, intelligent, and charming—a kind, generous man who was at one with everything that life had to offer. He took adventure as part of everyday life and embraced it joyously. Men of character liked him because of his courage and because he knew what he was talking about. In an attempt to let this Bror be heard by a new generation, I have collected the letters he wrote during his years in Africa. They are here made available in English for the first time.

Baron Bror Frederik von Blixen-Finecke and his twin brother Hans were born at the family estate in Näsbyholm, Sweden, in 1886. So close were they that they were hardly ever called by their own names; almost always they were referred to as "the twins." They were charmers from the start, though their constant pranks and their unwillingness to work hard at their lessons caused their parents some concern. But horses, dogs, hunting, and guns were also an essential part of the education of scions of titled families, and at these pursuits the boys excelled. Their family's estate had some of the best shooting in the country, and both became brilliant shots.

Having finished their schooling, Hans entered the cavalry and, until his untimely death in a flying accident in 1917, was regarded as Sweden's foremost gentleman rider. Bror attended agricultural college and was later appointed manager of a small estate near Näsbyholm. He was not a success in this role and one relative wrote "it appeared that Bror had large holes in all his pockets. He simply could not keep money and this unfortunate affliction never left him."

I knew Bror from my earliest childhood, for he lived on a small estate that he rented from his father, and we lived only a few hundred yards away. I first met Tanne (the name by which the family knew Karen) just after her engagement to Bror, when they visited Näsbyholm some time around 1913. I was about five years old then, and she made an enormously favorable impression on me, prepared as she was to spend a lot of time playing with me. Shortly after this, Bror sailed for East Africa, where, with money from both families, a dairy farm had been purchased.

Being the man he was, Bror was lucky to be born at the time he was, when there was still adventure to be had. When he traveled to British East Africa in 1913, he found a fantastic unspoiled wilderness, a Garden of Eden that had survived intact. It gave ample opportunity for a man of his talents to be himself, unfettered by the fixed conventions of European society. Life there demanded an adventurous spirit and an instinct for survival; it gave in return a freedom that today can only be dreamt of.

It was Bror's job to reconnoiter the country for its potential and to get the dairy farm going before Tanne joined him. It was not long, however, before he came to the conclusion that coffee farming would be more lucrative than dairy farming. So, with the approval of the investors—and Tanne—he sold the original farm and purchased a tract of land near Nairobi, where he built a farmhouse. In January 1914, Tanne arrived in East Africa, and the couple were married immediately in Mombasa before traveling in a private railway carriage up country to Nairobi.

Tanne was enchanted with the farmhouse and impressed with Bror's work. "I think it would give you great joy to hear how everyone I have met out here speaks about Bror," she wrote home shortly after her arrival. "Everyone without exception comes up to me and says that he has put in an exceptional piece of work on the farm and is an example for the whole of Africa."* Young, confident, and full of vitality, the couple enjoyed an idyllic existence at first. Money was plentiful, there were hunting and shooting safaris, merry parties to attend, and life was wonderful. But within months World War I was declared. Bror's nationality provoked a certain amount of suspicion among the English settlers, who wondered if Sweden would side with Germany and if the Swedish settlers in British East Africa would sympathize or even secretly aid the Germans in neighboring Tanganyika (later Tanzania). As a consequence, Bror made desperate though unsuccessful efforts to join the war effort on the side of the British. Eventually he was allowed to work with a scouting unit organized by Lord Delamere, one of the great pioneers of British East African settlement, but the unit was disbanded after a year.

The coffee farm never prospered. Although the rainfall and soil of Nairobi appeared to be similar to that of the well-established coffee-growing districts nearby, for example at Kiambu and Thika, the fact is that Bror and Tanne were the first to try planting coffee there. What would not become apparent until the coffee trees began to bear fruit some three or four years after planting was that the cold winds sweeping down from the Ngong hills at night had a disastrous effect on the trees at flowering time. As hard as they tried, Tanne and Bror were not able to grow coffee profitably at Ngong. Many other hopeful settlers in the emergent country, where crop experimentation was the order of the day, would also learn such hard lessons.

However, it is undeniable that a fundamental mistake had been made, at least in the scale chosen for what had been envisioned as an experimental farming exercise. With hindsight, it is easy to see that it would have been more prudent for the Blixens to have planted a smaller acreage and evaluated the results before giving their total commitment to the one crop. But they did not do so, and by the time it was realized that the crop had failed, the capital and patience of the backers, given the large initial outlays of both, had almost given out. Perhaps even more important for the young couple, things between them had begun to cool.

Much has been made of the fact that Tanne contracted venereal disease

---

*Isak Dinesen, Letters from Africa (Chicago: University of Chicago Press, 1981), pp. 3–4.

from Bror, causing her great pain and making it necessary for her to return to Denmark for extended treatment. There is no way to prove that she did indeed contract the disease from Bror, nor to prove that he ever, in fact, had it to give her. From most accounts, Bror was extremely healthy all his life and certainly never showed symptoms of advanced syphilis. According to Tanne's biographer, the disease runs different courses in different people, and so it is possible that Bror could have remained virtually symptomless while still having passed the disease onto Tanne, who suffered greatly. However, Bror's subsequent wives and lovers (and admittedly there were many) vehemently deny that he had the disease. Nor is there a suggestion anywhere that he passed the illness on to anyone else. Nonetheless, Tanne's illness was clearly a tragedy for them both.

Although no person outside a marriage really knows why it fails, I strongly believe that the marriage may have come to an end as the result of nothing more profound than the incompatibility between them caused by their different mental and emotional makeups. He was a extrovert, a doer. She was a poet and a dreamer. Added to this was the necessity of having to face up to a financial crisis, which neither of them was particularly equipped to cope with. The combination ultimately proved fatal to their marriage.

At the height of their problems came word of the sudden and tragic death in 1917 of Bror's twin brother Hans, who, together with his co-pilot, had been killed when the engine of their airplane failed. This loss must have rocked Bror to the roots, and though no one can say precisely what effect it had on his ability to face his day-to-day problems, it certainly must have been profoundly painful and unsettling.

As their relationship cooled, Tanne and Bror went their separate ways. Tanne fell in love with the country, the Africans, the farm, and the game. Later she was to meet Denys Finch Hatton and would enjoy a remarkable love affair with him. But in the main she lived in her own way, working, writing, studying, and absorbing all that was around her—a route that led to the remarkable woman she became.

Bror's love for East Africa was no less passionate than Tanne's, though his took a different, more active, form. Bror craved adventure and constant excitement. The tedium involved in maintaining an established (though failing) farm quickly destroyed Bror's enthusiasm for the project. He spent more and more time away from home, wandering around the country and engaging in hunting exploits. He was a born hunter and an instinctive naturalist. These assets, together with an explorer's natural curiosity, made it inevitable that he would get to know the country intimately. He was always searching for new game areas, bigger game, and learning more about the uncharted wilderness in which he had chosen to make his life. He had a marvelous eye for land and for livestock, and he introduced many clients and friends to farm sites that later flourished and made money. Ironically, he could never perform this miracle for himself.

Another of Bror's assets was his devastating charm, to which both sexes succumbed. Women were particularly fascinated by him and openly pursued him all his life. In a moralizing tone Bror has been depicted as a pursuer of women. Nothing could be more untrue or ridiculous. Women turned to him as the most natural thing in the world and he never had to do the chasing. He loved the company of women and displayed great courtesy and gentleness in his dealings with them. It is hardly surprising that each woman rapidly gained the impression that she was the only one who mattered to Bror, or that many said later that they would never forget him. As for Bror, he "fell in love" frequently, and on every occasion he thought, "this is the real thing." Whenever this happened, everything else became of secondary importance. So when, in the early twenties, Bror met and fell in love with a married lady—the pretty and witty Cockie Birkbeck—he asked Tanne for a divorce.

Tanne was distressed at his request. Despite the fact that Bror no longer lived with her, it was perfectly acceptable to her that she and Bror should pursue their respective lives but remain married in name. Bror was a constant visitor to the farm and, until he and Cockie married, enjoyed an openly friendly relationship with Tanne. Her family, however, felt differently about him. They were appalled at his record as husband and provider, and laid the farm's failure directly at his door. Tanne was told that the backers would continue to invest in the farm only on the conditions that Bror never be allowed to set foot on the property again and that a formal divorce be instituted. In those days, she wrote often to my mother, who was Bror's eldest sister, and in one letter she stated her position on the dissolution of her marriage: "As far as I am concerned, I can only say that I am inexpressively fond of Bror and it would for me be the greatest sorrow in the world to be divorced from him. I know very well that I by no means have been a good wife to him, but I do not think that there is anybody in the world who is as fond of him as I am."

What has not always been made quite clear is that Bror lost everything he owned in the farm's failure. Although Tanne's family had made the major investment, Bror also sank his entire personal wealth into the farm and when he was banned from its precincts he became a penniless wanderer, literally left with the clothes in which he stood and living on the charity of his many friends.

He was, it must be admitted, hopeless with money and a despair to his creditors. Once, even before Cockie and Bror were married, in order to settle his debts Cockie was reduced to offering her pearls to a tradesman who was threatening to imprison Bror. Despite this, Bror was liked by everyone for his easygoing and sunny nature. Tradespeople, dhuka-wallahs, and tribal chiefs, farmers, lawyers, and the socially elite "Happy Valley" set: all succumbed to his charm. As for Bror himself, he was equally at home in the company of royalty, or in high society (where he was renowned for capping brilliant conversation with pieces of killing understatement), as he was sleeping in a ditch. He was fascinating to listen to, and was more widely read than one might have expected from such an obvious man of action, and now he became universally known by his nickname, Blix, the name I have always called him.

Once, in the early twenties, when his creditors were at last reduced to serving a writ on him, Blix vanished, living on the run in the open countryside. In the meantime his friends got together, reached an arrangement with the creditors for a much reduced figure, and settled the amount among them. It is part of the old Kenya legend that during this period, while officially in hiding from the law, Blix was seen, perfectly attired in full evening dress as the personal guest of the governor, General Northey, at an official Government House function.

Always a popular guest, Blix had a remarkable capacity for alcohol, though he was never the worse for it. His stamina was astonishing and one friend recalls how, after a traditional three-day New Year's celebration at the Muthaiga Club, which included "racing, dancing and feasting—during which time nobody got any sleep—he suddenly left early in the morning to prepare a camp on the Serengeti, ready to receive a party of Safari clients who were arriving by air that same day."

Eventually, Blix and Cockie married, dooming any hope of a continued open and friendly relationship with Tanne. Cockie, who now lives near Newbury in England, claims "Tania never forgave me for what she saw as 'stealing' Bror away from her." Although Cockie came from a well-connected family and had been raised in a rather grand manner in England, she had no money of her own. Her father, a rich banker, had often told the family that when he died nothing would be left. Living in great affluence, the family quite naturally took this as a joke and were appalled to find upon his death that he had spoken the truth. The newlyweds were therefore quite without resources and when a friend, Dick Cooper, offered congratulations, saying to Cockie, "I hope you'll be very happy," her reply was, "So do I, but it may be difficult without a penny to our names."

Cooper's response was to offer the couple £800 a year to go to Babati in Tanganyika and plant coffee on a parcel of land (later Singu Estates) for which he had recently been granted a lease. It was a hard life. Before they could begin to farm they had to clear the bush and build a shack in which to live. Their only water supply was rainwater collected from their corrugated tin roof. In the rainy season, though, they had so much water that they were often marooned for weeks at a time. Still, Cockie recalls these years as the happiest in her life.

Why? the reader might ask, when they were faced with such hardships. A difficult question to answer. I myself could give no concrete reasons why a certain period in my life was the happiest. Herewith, however, are some factors that might explain her point of view. The financial crisis that followed in the wake of the Wall Street collapse and swept over the U.S. and Europe in the late twenties and early thirties came to East Africa in 1930; everybody was short of cash. It is always easier to be poor when most of one's friends have similar difficulties. Cockie was living with a husband whom she loved. They were both pioneers, having been given the task of establishing a new farm in a new area on a site that was quite possibly the most beautiful I've seen in Africa. Building a house, making a garden, et cetera, all made life well worth living. There was good hunting and birdshooting on their doorstep. Friends from Kenya and Europe frequently came motoring or flying down to see them. Cockie loved to play bridge, and there was plenty of that. Because of Dick Cooper's backing, there was a measure of financial security. Also, there was no resident female competition, and the climate was superb. In short, why shouldn't Cockie have been happy?

Cockie is an immensely generous person, but in bridge she could be a bit avaricious. Bror once had invited her cousin Jerry Alexander from Molo and his mother to come down and stay at Singu. On their arrival the bridge table was already prepared, and they were made to play for the next three days from nine A.M. to midnight. The arrangement was not quite fair, as Cockie insisted on having me as a permanent partner. At that time contract bridge was fairly new in Kenya, but Cockie and I had played it quite a lot in Europe. The Alexanders were beginners, and I doubt if they enjoyed their stay, since they eventually left quite a bit poorer. On another occasion Blix and I had gone to Moshi to attend a funeral, leaving Cockie in Arusha, the nearest large town. When the funeral was over I got a telephone call from Cockie, asking me to return to Arusha forthwith. It seems she had been out the night before playing bridge, with the result that she was obliged to leave a check behind, and this would have to be retrieved before the bank opened on Monday morning. This was done and the check was exchanged for another one in our favor. (Incidentally, Cockie had many meetings with the bank manager, a dour Scotsman named Dunn. She usually left him with the words "Dunn again.")

Because of his superior knowledge of the bush, flora and fauna, Blix was soon in great demand as a white hunter by the growing number of safari parties then flocking to East Africa. Not surprisingly, he was asked by Finch Hatton to take part in both of the safaris made by the Prince of Wales. Later, he was one of the first to use airplanes for spotting game and was friends with and employed well-known bush pilots—Tom Campbell Black, Fatty Pearson, and the remarkable Beryl Markham (who in her book *West with the Night* aptly described the Kenya of those days as "days of toil and nights of gladness") among them.

Obviously the first qualification for a white hunter is that he be a first-class shot, and Blix was certainly that. I can recall helping him practice by throwing small sticks as high into the air as I could. Using a .22 rifle and swinging it like a shotgun, Blix hit his mark a good seventy-five percent of the time. But in order to achieve the reputation that he did as a great white hunter, much more than rifle skills were needed. Great organizational ability was required to ensure in the middle of the bush a camp equipped to the rather high standard of comfort demanded by his wealthy safari clients; Blix had the quality in abundance. And though he may have sat up most of the previous night entertaining clients (consuming a fair amount of alcoholic beverage in the process), he was always alert early next morning, calling his often huge staff together—second hunters, camp manager, mechanic, pilot, head boy, et cetera—to give them a briefing and instructions for the day's safari.

An unrivaled knowledge of the country and the ways of game were also essential to ensure that clients went home with the trophies they sought. Blix had a passion for elephant hunting. He considered elephants the most fascinating and interesting animals in Africa and was always searching for big "tuskers." But he became most famous for his ability to track and produce lions for his paying guns. Even in areas where lions were scarce, Blix could generally be relied upon to find one, and it was for this reason that Finch Hatton asked him to join the prince's safari. (Perhaps Blix's contentment with his new wife and his happy-go-lucky life of hunting made him oblivious to the manner in which he and Cockie lived. When he took the Prince of Wales home one day for breakfast he was startled and embarrassed when the prince took him to one side and said, "I say, Blixen, you oughn't to let your wife live in a tumbledown place like this!")

There was yet another desirable quality that a white hunter needed: the ability to manage the huge teams of Africans who acted as porters and beaters on safaris. Blix understood and liked Africans, and they worked for him and gave him their loyalty in a way that they did for few other white men. They not only liked him, they respected him and his knowledge, and called him *Waboga* ("the Wild Goose"), perhaps because of his constant travels. Farah Aden, who figured so prominently in Tanne's book and in the film *Out of Africa*, and whom I knew extremely well, once told me that in this world he only greatly respected one God and two mortals. The three were Allah, and the Baron and Baroness Blixen.

Last, a good white hunter never underestimated the dangers of the safari. Bror once told me it was very difficult to convey to visiting clients how much care was needed, or how quickly the hunter could become the hunted. He also said (more out of self-deprecation than total accuracy) that seventy-five percent of a white hunter's role was to be a glorified butler and to keep the client amused.

Blix's travels were many. There was a period of exile in Uganda and the Congo that he spent hunting. Later, he met Sir Charles Markham and the two not only became firm friends but made the first crossings of the Sahara in a four-wheeled vehicle. When he made periodic visits to his family in Sweden I was an avid listener to his stories of the good life in Africa. As I was not tempted to pursue further advanced studies and had no prospects of acquiring a farm of my own, the idea of emigrating became more and more attractive to me. Finally, in 1931, I left to join Uncle, who readily agreed with me that I was not well equipped to succeed in the rat race at home. (Actually what he said was, "You're too bloody stupid, my boy!")

When I first arrived in East Africa, I spent a year on the farm in Tanganyika with Blix and Cockie. In the immediate vicinity of the farm there was very good buffalo shooting, and we frequently went out together for an afternoon's hunt. He taught me everything I now know about this particular animal—how it behaves when hunted and when wounded. Above all he stressed the extreme danger to the hunter from the buffalo. He and I stayed in constant touch for the rest of his time in Africa, often going on safaris together. The relationship at first was that of uncle and nephew, but gradually it developed into a close personal friendship, one that gave me many happy memories.

Blix's marriage to Cockie failed in 1933 and he soon fell in love with an attractive Swede named Eva Dickson. Despite her glamor and an adventurous nature, Eva was neither accepted nor admired by Blix's friends, who disliked her ability to dominate him. Although she called herself Baroness Blixen, Blix once confided to me that they had never formally married. Blix's attitude was, "If it amuses her to call herself Baroness, let her do so." (Unfortunately, Eva, who had been eavesdropping at the door, heard Blix's quiet confidence and came storming into the room accusing Blix of not being able to keep a secret and of breaking his word.)

Eva was in Sweden in 1936 when Blix flew to England with Beryl Markham, who had become one of his staunchest friends. In her memoir written in 1942, Beryl devoted several chapters to hunting and flying adventures with him, and it is interesting to read her assessment of his personality. "Blix . . . is six feet of amiable Swede and, to my knowledge, the toughest, most durable white hunter ever to snicker at the fanfare of safari or to shoot a charging buffalo between the eyes while debating whether his sundown drink will be gin or whisky." Describing her welcome on one occasion when she flew into his camp, she writes:

> . . . The aristocratically descended visage of the Baron von Blixen Finecke greeted me (as it always did) with the most delightful of smiles caught, like a strip of sunlight, on a familiar patch of leather—well-kept leather, free of wrinkles but brown and saddle-tough. Beyond this concession to the fictional idea of what a white hunter ought to look like Blix's face yields not a whit. He has merry, light blue eyes rather than sombre, steel grey ones; his cheeks are well-rounded rather than flat as an axe; his lips are full and generous and not pinched tight in grim realization of What the Wilderness Can Do. He talks. He is never significantly silent.
>
> He wore then what I always remember him wearing, a khaki bush shirt of "solario" material, slacks of the same stuff and a pair of low-cut moccasins with soles—or at least vestiges of soles.

There were four pockets in his bush shirt but I don't think he knew it; he never carried anything unless he was actually hunting—and then it was just a rifle and ammunition. He never went around hung with knives, revolvers, binoculars, or even a watch. He could tell the time by the sun, and if there were no sun he could tell it anyway. He wore over his close-cropped greying hair a terai hat, colourless and limp as a wilted frond.*

It has many times been suggested that Beryl and Blix had a love affair. I knew both of them very well at the time concerned, and as far as I know, there was never a romance between them. Still, when they were both out on reconnaissance safaris they quite naturally—neither of them being a great believer in celibacy—found it more entertaining not to sleep alone. They were very good friends and enjoyed an easy-going, carefree relationship with many shared interests, including a deep love for East Africa, an unrivaled knowledge of its animals and wilderness, and a taste for adventure.

What is true is that Beryl recognized Blix as a great personality, and in that she was not alone. Many people, including Blix's great friend Ernest Hemingway, shared her opinion. A recent article in *The New York Times* stated that Blix was the model for Hemingway's macho white-hunter character, Robert Wilson, in "The Short and Happy Life of Francis Macomber"; however, Hemingway's offical biographer, Carlos Baker, disagrees. He believes that Wilson was based on Philip Percival. Perhaps the truth is that the character of Wilson was drawn from the real-life adventures of both men. In Mary Hemingway's *How It Was* (Ballantine, 1976), there are a number of anecdotes about Blix and his adventures, which clearly stimulated Hemingway's fertile imagination. Blix's perspective was wide, and small-mindedness (and by that I do not mean narrow-mindedness) was completely foreign to him. No problem was too difficult for him to tackle. Perhaps his greatest faults were a tendency to trade unwittingly on his charm and the fact that at times his unfailing generosity led him into actions that could be described as irresponsible.

At Blix's request, I once joined one of his safaris as camp manager. It was possibly one of the most luxurious safaris that has ever been outfitted, and was paid for by Alfred Vanderbilt's mother and superbly organized

---

*Beryl Markham, *West with the Night* (San Francisco: North Point Press, 1983), p. 209.

and arranged by Blix. I seem to remember there being about fifteen clients, and large numbers of staff, employees, and transport, including a permanently attached aircraft and pilot. It was all very impressive.

Some time after that, in 1938, Blix suggested that we should make a new route along the Voi River down to the Mombasa–Malindi road, and also take the opportunity to shoot some big elephants, before I left for Europe by boat. A man called Graham Beech joined us, and we both had to promise Uncle that we wouldn't fire at anything under 120 pounds per tusk. After about a fortnight's fruitless search, I saw what I thought were a pair of very big tusks one morning. My tracker and I sat looking at the animal for more than an hour before I decided to take a chance. Admittedly the body was smallish, but this is always misleading when trying to judge the weight of the ivory. Later that evening we were sitting round the drinks table by the fire when the tusks were brought in. I glanced at Uncle, who, at times, had a fierce temper that he found difficult to control. A sure sign that such an outburst was imminent was when his somewhat prominent cheeks began to wobble. Sure enough, on this occasion, as I watched anxiously, the cheeks began to wobble. "You have broken your promise," he finally accused me angrily. Still worse was his dismissive summing up: "Toothpicks!"

Fortunately for me, however, the tusks wouldn't have been very handy for that purpose, as they weighed in at just under 110 pounds per tusk, and no more elephants were shot on that safari, which proved to be Blix's last one ever in Africa. When we finally arrived at our destination by Mariakani station, Blix decided that some celebration of my impending departure should be held and I was instructed to send for my current girlfriend, advise her to bring suitable female company and provisions both solid and liquid. Everything duly arrived, but during the night we were all disturbed by the dreaded soldier ant, which invaded our tents en masse.

In cases like this there is only one thing to do, and that is to get your clothes off as quickly as possible and scrape off the terrifying insects, which are capable of killing a horse or ox within hours. The only light we could see in the vicinity was the station master's office, and this was swiftly invaded by a completely unclothed party of Europeans. This so shocked the Indian station master that he rapidly left his office and retired to his quarters. Needless to say, no more train traffic signals were sent that night.

The following day, Blix asked me to do him a favor when I arrived in England. It seems he had been increasingly disturbed by the infiltration of

Germans into Tanganyika. Supported by Hitler and his regime, these German settlers had for the past couple of years slowly and methodically been buying not only land but also businesses and banks. Bror wanted the British to be aware of this and even went so far as to suggest that the cheapest and perhaps only way for the British government to regain control would be to arrange for a forced sale of all German-held property. There was only one man in England who would understand the situation, Blix told me, and that was Winston Churchill, whom he knew. To my lasting regret I failed to meet Churchill but did manage to see Duff Cooper, who was sympathetic but unresponsive; understandably perhaps when so many greater issues were mounting up. This was my last meeting with Blix in Africa. Soon thereafter he left for Europe, where we met briefly, before he departed to take up a job as Winston Guest's estate manager on Gardiner's Island at the eastern end of Long Island.

For some time previous to this, Blix's well-honed hunting instinct had started to dull and he began to prefer shooting with the camera. No member of the White Hunter's Association liked to take out clients whose chief aim was simply to slaughter as many animals as possible. Indeed the professional white hunter was—in this respect—the greatest possible help to the game department in seeing that the licensing laws were strictly adhered to. In view of this, there are some passages in the letters that follow that readers may find puzzling. For example, when Blix describes his joy at seeing lions at play before he shoots them, this latter action seems to me to be at odds with his general outlook. Much more in keeping with my knowledge of his attitude toward animals is his meeting with the cobra. "Why shoot? It had given me an honest warning and asked me to leave. . . ." The only explanation seems to be a necessity to keep the fee-paying client happy.

In earlier years, though, he had loved "la chasse" and, having shot practically every species—when animals were so numerous that no one gave conservation a second thought—he came to the conclusion that he got the most excitement out of hunting buffalo and elephant. The buffalo has very good eyesight (when he charges, he does so with his head raised, watching you all the time), good hearing, and a good sense of smell. When he knows he is being hunted he will make a well-thought-out plan as to how to either avoid you or destroy you. A challenge. The elephant has poor eyesight but is compensated by very highly developed senses of smell and hearing. By virtue of his very size, the elephant is awe inspiring and a most formidable adversary.

There were two types of elephant hunting in Bror's day. The first involved tracking the big tusker. This was wholly fascinating, for you were always on the alert, starting at dawn, and sleeping on the track at night. Blix also did quite a bit of another kind of elephant hunting, what is called elephant control, i.e., moving the elephant population from one part of the country to another. This was always done on government orders as part of an overall attempt to free a particular district from sleeping sickness, which is spread by the tsetse fly, an insect that requires shade to live. First large areas are cleared from bush and the natives are encouraged to grow crops to keep the wild vegetation down. They will do so unless elephants arrive, for elephant herds will eat and trample down crops. Soon, the native departs, the bush grows up again, in comes the tsetse, and the circle is complete.

Hunters on elephant control worked without license but had to turn over to the game department half the ivory they obtained. If you were assigned an area of very thick bush, with visibility limited to a few feet and very big herds in the area (up to several hundred animals, mostly cows and calves), you found yourself in probably the most dangerous type of hunting situation that exists. The elephant soon gets to know what it's all about, and when the sun gets low in the late afternoon, he starts hunting you instead of vice versa. The sight and sound of a large herd of infuriated, screaming cows in full charge is terrifying. I tried it once for a month in very thick country near Lake Victoria and decided that was quite enough. I once spent six months with some friends on the Uganda–Sudan border, when we averaged thirty miles a day.

Not surprisingly, this kind of hunting appealed to Blix more than any other. In effect you declare war on your adversary, and the farther you have to walk to get to him the more intensified does this private battle become. You often track one animal for more than a week.

His book *Nyama* (published as *African Hunter* in England and America) has some interesting passages in it but leaves much unsaid. Beryl Markham, in her own book, stated: "If Blix has ever yielded to embarrassment before any situation, it must have been when he confronted himself with writing his all too shy record of his work in Africa. The book, to those who knew him is a monument of understatement. In it he has made molehills out of all the mountains he has climbed, and passed off as incidents true stories that a less modest man might enlarge to blood-curdling sagas." As a matter of fact Blix did not personally write that book—he employed a ghostwriter whose only recompense for the task was that he could drink as much champagne as he could consume during the writing process.

Blix enjoyed his few years on Gardiner's Island. He had many friends and was a welcome guest at numerous parties. His days were full and happy as he worked to keep the island well-stocked with wildfowl and pheasants for visiting guns. He had an elderly Turkish couple who looked after him devotedly, and his remarkable knowledge of nature enabled him to breed the birds with great success. However, when World War II was declared all this was put behind him.

Together with a young American girl, Polly Peabody, he raised money from wealthy New Yorkers to fund a medical relief organization backed by the Red Cross and sailed for occupied Finland. Landing in Norway, the party only just made it across the border into Sweden before Norway's occupation. Negotiating a narrow mountain pass on packed ice, the expedition was strafed by German fighter planes, but eventually a field hospital was set up. His part in this operation complete, Blix then joined up with a splinter group who went to fight in northern Norway. This did not last, however, and though he tried desperately and repeatedly to get to England to join in the fighting, he was always refused permission to travel. Eventually, dispirited, he returned to Skåne, not far from Ystad on the southern coast of Sweden, where he lived out the remainder of the war, somewhat bitter at what he saw as a rejection. He was a natural leader and would have made an excellent officer if he had been given the opportunity (though I feel he would have made a better commanding officer than a second-in-command). He was very courageous without being foolhardy and whenever posed with a problem he would never rest until the difficulties were overcome. A challenge—any challenge—had to be accepted and won.

A friend who knew Blix during his time with the Red Cross relief organization and later on in Sweden wrote:

. . . What immediately struck you at a first meeting was that he in no way corresponded with the normally accepted cliché of a "white hunter" as a sort of "he man" in films of these days.

At first he gave you the impression of being a somewhat grey and ordinary person. Grey hair, grey suit, grey-blue eyes. But as soon as he began to talk this notion changed radically. At once his charisma and very special sense of humour became apparent. I don't think I ever have met a more genuine person, so totally lacking in affectation and conceit. He was always the same, whether he talked to a five-year-old child or to a venerable old lady; with a Danish game-keeper in idiomatic Danish or with a British diplomat in perfect English.

Always softspoken and untroubled in all situations and always with that indescribable humour which was such a big part of his charm. He may have been a bit slap-dash at times, and something of a bohemian in many ways, but he was a personality. He had a sort of poise, and exuded security and harmony, which was surprising when at times one knew that he had only one suit of clothes in his wardrobe.

He had many friends and I don't believe he had a single enemy. Those who knew him in Africa can tell about how much he was liked by his employees, and I'm sure his sense of humour must have greatly contributed to this. In any company where Bror was present, everything became pleasant and as a matter of course, without any urge of self-assertion, he became the centre of attention.*

It was toward the end of the war that a second book was published in Sweden under the title *Brev Från Afrika (Letters from Africa)*, consisting of a series of letters. It is these letters, which I have now translated and offer here, together with previously unpublished letters Blix wrote to his sister (which I have also translated), that make up *Bror Blixen: The Africa Letters*. Of those letters translated from *Brev Från Afrika*, some are known to be edited and adapted from letters originally written to Cockie or Dick Cooper. Although it has been stated in a recent biography of Karen that most of these letters were written to Eva, with the exception of the last letter, this is incorrect. Most of them cover a period in the twenties and thirties before Blix met Eva.

Others, however, were not written as letters per se. As was the literary tradition at that time, these letters were epistolary letters; that is, Blix wrote letters that he might have written to Cockie or Dick, simply as a means of telling his stories. This enabled him to present them in a more personal way than had been possible in *Nyama*, and he could relate the stories without appearing to brag about his role in them.

Although these letters are primarily about hunting, Blix's perceptive

---

*Letter written by Gosta Adelsward.

views of the country and its inhabitants, both human and animal, are fascinating ones. He was not a writer in the way that Tanne was a writer, or that Beryl Markham or Ernest Hemingway were writers. But he does bring to his work the sense that here is a man who really knows and loves his subject. It is easy to feel his sense of absolute belonging to the wonderful country that was East Africa.

Today, with dwindling wild animal populations, the world looks upon hunting with a different eye. But when Blix hunted in East Africa there were countless numbers of animals and no one thought there was anything wrong in the hunting of them. The African tribespeople certainly viewed it favorably and saw the killing of an elephant or buffalo as cause for great rejoicing and feasting; for them it meant a welcome store of meat for the foreseeable future. But hunting necessarily led Blix to discover and learn more and more about the animals themselves, and he shares some of this immense knowledge in these letters, so that—even if the thought of hunting appalls you—you will find interest in his literary attempts to sketch his way of life. (Incidentally, Blix's knowledge of animal husbandry formed a large part of the basis for the game laws in East Africa.)

The last time I saw Blix was when, in the summer of 1945, I was on leave from a posting in Burma (where I had met up with our old friend Fatty Pearson, also mentioned in these letters). I was staying with Blix in Skåne, where he was then living with his last great love, Ruth Rasmussøn. It was perhaps the first time he had achieved a completely harmonious love and happiness with a woman. They were running a small poultry farm and kennels and seemed very happy and content, but Blix worried about not taking an active part in the war and obviously thought that feeding chickens and exercising dogs were not exactly the highlight of his adventurous life. Still, we spent many hours talking about our times in Africa and Blix mentioned they were planning to return there as soon as travel was possible. It was only after I returned to active duty that I heard of Blix's death in a car accident on Easter Sunday, 1946.

I saw Tanne sometimes, including once in the mid-thirties when I spent a short time at home and she came to visit my mother. Our conversation then was mostly about happy African reminiscences. The last time I saw her was at Rungstedlund, where I visited her in 1959. We embraced and I promised to call again but sadly I was recalled to Africa sooner than expected, so I was unable to keep my promise. She was truly a fantastic person. Her imagination was limitless and, as an author and an artist, she has—in my opinion—few equals in our generation. At no time did she ever refer to Blix or their life together with anything even vaguely suggesting unpleasantness.

Much has been written about East Africa but there is one piece of text that I particularly like, for to me it epitomizes the Africa I knew and that I shared with Blix. It was written by Teddy Roosevelt and used by Murray Smith in the foreword to his book *The Nature of the Beast* (Jarrolds, 1963):

> . . . There are no words that can tell the hidden spirit of the wilderness, that can reveal its mystery, its melancholy, its charm. There is a delight in the hardy life in the open, in the thrill of the fight with dangerous game. Apart from this, yet mingled with it, is the strong attraction of the silent plains, of the great tropic moons, of the splendour of the new stars; where the wanderer sees the awful glory of sunset and sunrise, in the wide spans of the earth, unworn of man, and changed only by the slow passing of the ages through time everlasting. . . .

Stirring words and hard to improve upon.

—G. F. V. Kleen
Drottningholm
February 1988

CHAPTER

1

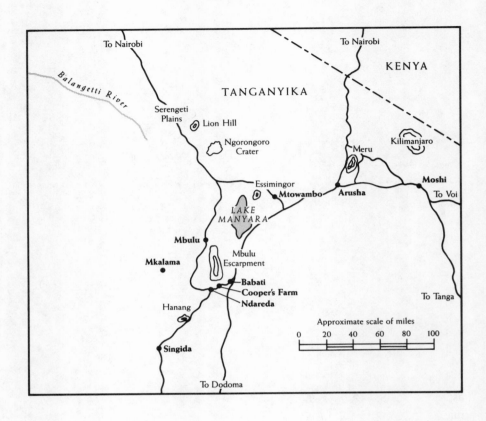

·····································

Swedo African Coffee Co. Ltd
M'ruru Estate, Ngong
Box 130, PO Nairobi

Telegrams Address "Coffeeries"

15/7/1913

My dear Ellen,*
Very many thanks for your letter. I really think it is I who should feel
ashamed for writing so seldom, and not you. So far, I believe I've only
managed to write to you once. In spite of the fact that the mail doesn't
leave for another week I'll start replying to your letter today, as there is
always so much to write about at the last moment.
Such a pity that you were unable to move into Truedsons' villa this year,
as you all had such a good time there last summer. I quite understand that
you are worried about Thyra's recurring colds and her impaired hearing
and your first consideration must be to follow the advice of the doctor and
to go wherever he thinks it is best for her. It is a pity though that you
won't be able to go with Dad, and Ebba and her children, to Falmouth,
which you had so much been looking forward to. Unfortunately, a ticket
for a voyage out here is quite expensive, otherwise I could have been
looking forward to embracing the entire family at Kilindini. Your stay out
here wouldn't have cost very much. I myself feel better than ever, but
otherwise the health situation on the farm is not too good. Holmberg is
suffering from sunstroke, Rundgren and most of the Africans are down
with smallpox, so I suppose it's only a matter of time before I catch it. Mr.

---

*Bror's elder sister.

Grieve accidentally shot himself in the face a couple of days ago, which has not improved his already untidy appearance. Two cows and two oxen died last night with what the veterinary officer who had been sent for diagnosed as East Coast fever, one of the virulent cattle pests we have to contend with.

However, I am as fit as a fiddle, bursting with good health, and really appreciating the splendors of Africa. It is difficult to define exactly what it is that makes life out here so enjoyable—maybe it is being so far away from all gossip and nagging, living on ground which has never been ploughed, walking in forests that have never experienced saw or axe, and above all the wide open spaces and the great tempting possibilities that lie ahead. A country still in its infancy and which on the strength of its fertility and excellent climate invites pioneering. It is my belief that apart from farming, it would be prudent to invest in anything here that is profitable at home such as hotels, bookshops, et cetera, et cetera.

Mummy wrote in her last letter about Soeberg that it might be wise to invest that money here, and I cannot but agree with such an idea. By buying uncultivated land now, and then sometime in the future selling it as an established farm, one would be certain to make a substantial profit. I think it would be a good idea if all of you contributed to the fare for somebody wise, like Gustaf Hamilton,* to come out here with a view to making an economic survey of the potential. There would be no risk of losing money, as the value of land increases every month. The worst that could possibly happen would be that some terrible epidemic struck down the indigenous population, and as there are some 3 million of them this is hardly likely, since their standard of living is now rising with better employment and modernized medical aid.

I have had a letter from Uncle Mogens,† who wanted to know more about MacMillan's farm, but as he has by now got this information from Sjögren, there is no need for an immediate answer.

20/7/1913

I'll finish this letter quickly, as I've got a letter from Westenholz which I have to reply to and also write to Tanne, so please tell Mummy that she'll only hear from me by the next mail; in the meantime, will you please thank her from me for her long letter.

---

*One of Blix's brother-in-laws.
†Blix's mother's brother, Count Frijs.

I got the letter from Westenholz when I was out in the bush, hunting with Holmberg and Rundgren since Friday (today is Sunday). We saw a lot of game of all varieties. I got a good impala and a waterbuck, and I had to leave them today in order to get these letters off with tomorrow's mail. I departed, having strapped a duiker I had just shot onto the saddle, and rode home. Suddenly another duiker jumped out from some scrub, and I fired but muffed the shot. The horse reared with the crack of the shot and turned. When I had regained my balance, I saw something else moving in the long grass and, with the field glasses, I could see a lioness sitting up, carefully observing my movements.

I quickly dismounted, but the range was a little too far, over three hundred yards, and I could only see the head. I crawled on hands and knees towards her, and it looked promising, as she did the same, but soon she sat down again, and since I now had come to a stony ledge, I could no longer hide myself in the grass. The situation was precarious as we sat studying each other, and I watched her with the glasses for a few minutes. Never before had I seen such an insolent and defiant expression on the face of an animal. A lion in a cage could never be compared to that free and self-assured beast. I retracted the bolt of the rifle and found to my consternation that it was empty. In my pocket, I only had two cartridges, one soft-nosed and one solid. Which one was I going to fire first? I decided to put the soft-nosed in the breech and the other one in the magazine.* Another look in the glasses, and then suddenly she disappeared, as if swallowed by the earth.

After a couple of minutes she reappeared, her tail straight up in the air, then lashing her sides with it and advancing a few paces. Then she sat down again, fixing me with that threatening stare. I changed the two bullets in the rifle, but her head was now completely obscured in the sights and I couldn't get a satisfactory aim. Following the general advice of never firing too early, I calmed myself down a bit, but the time passed slowly and the situation did not change. There was a dried-out tree to the left and I crawled towards it, to use it as a support. All the time her truculent gaze followed me and, as if she at last had realized the danger she was now in, she crouched down in the grass just as I was ready to fire. I saw her crawling into the thicket.

In the glasses I could just see her outline amongst the undergrowth, but with the naked eye it was impossible. I again changed the cartridges

---

*The wrong decision, I feel. GFVK.

around, advanced towards her, rounded the bushes, fetched the horse, stayed there for another half hour, and now am sitting here without having got another glimpse of her. However, I've seen a lion, and the proud and calm bearing of this powerful animal is something I'll never forget.

Give my love to everybody at home,

In haste, your own affectionate,
Bror

Mombasa Club
East Africa
13/1/1914

My dear Ellen,

Like all other letters I have written to you I shall have to start this one
by apologizing for your not having heard from me earlier.

I am sitting in the Mombasa Club, where I am staying, and it is very
pleasant. The waves are coming in only a few yards below me and there is
a beautiful garden with palm trees and ornamental bushes. Compared to
Nairobi, Mombasa is a very much more attractive town; you don't find the
bustle and noise that is already prevalent in the capital. And of course
there is the nearness to the ocean. Here, more than anywhere else, one
gets a feeling of complete relaxation. Tomorrow at two P.M. Tanne will
arrive with Prince William, Bostrom, and Lewenhaupt.

As you will understand, I am now about to embark on a new and important phase of my life. I can't think of anything more pleasant than to
receive one's fiancée under these conditions—to start an entirely new way
of life, with new conventions and practices, in a new country with a
different population. Unfortunately, our house isn't quite ready yet; there
are still Indian craftsmen busily finishing off the painting and interior
decoration, but in a week's time everything should be completed. In the
meantime I'll take her up to Naivasha, where I have work to do on Uncle
Mogen's land, and there she'll get a chance to get fully rested from her
voyage.

This is one of the more picturesque places in East Africa, and I am
sending her horse up there so that she'll get the opportunity of being able
to ride around and get a first impression of the country. I am hoping to be

able to arrange a lion hunt for her with Paul Rainey's Rhodesian Ridgeback dogs, as I believe this would be a wonderful introduction to African life—that is if she feels up to it. I have selected, out of the one thousand farm employees, the fifteen tallest Kavirondo, all over 6 ft., as her personal suite.

I have called on the Governor, who was very helpful and gave us a carriage on the special train which had been put at the disposal of the Prince and invited us to the lunch the following day at Government House after our arrival in Nairobi. MacMillan and Sjögren are here to meet His Royal Highness, and after his arrival in Nairobi it is planned that they should all go out to MacMillan's place and from there hunt for about six weeks—after that nothing definite has been planned.

Luckily, I am, as always, feeling very fit and the climate seems to suit me. It looks, however, as if Rundgren will soon have to return home if he is not to waste away to nothing. My man Holmberg is also losing weight and his wife, who came out with the last boat, is now in hospital with malaria. Miss Donkin, completely worn out, will be leaving for England on Saturday, so it looks as though the altitude and the sun have an adverse effect on some people.

Miss Donkin has been here for many years. I've given her your summer address in Falmouth and if she happens to be near there at any time she'll probably look you up and could describe what the farm looks like, et cetera. She's visited me several times.

I often think of you and your children and I imagine the young ones are looking forward to the summer by the beach. By now I suppose Thyra is quite fluent in English. Next year I really hope Daddy comes out here instead. After all, it's quite a comfortable voyage; I'm sure it would interest him to see the country and besides he has promised to come. It's not at all hot in Nairobi, so he needn't worry about that. One uses four blankets at night. He won't have to walk, he can either get about by riding a horse or by being driven. The bathroom is now ready, so that ought to tempt him!

The farming is progressing in a satisfactory manner and there will be quite an area prepared for the coffee planting in the long rains during March-April, probably a hundred and fifty acres. I am very pleased that Westenholz is coming out by the end of May. I have got one thousand boys working and hope to be able to keep up this number by self-recruiting. I have been promised that permission will be granted for an extension of the railway line. Westenholz will have to decide.

Give my love to everybody and kiss the children for me.

Your affectionate,
Bror

P.S. I don't think I've thanked you for the gramophone. What a wonderful present. There are sixteen cases waiting for me in Customs and, as there are no invoices, they all have to be opened.

· ·

Ndareda
Nov 1930

My darling Cockie,*

This morning through my field glasses I saw a herd of buffalo grazing just above our proposed house site and further beyond—by the great granite block which you remember—stood two elephants busily breaking down trees in order to get at the tender top branches.

The formerly burnt-out plains have changed color and now present themselves in the pale green of spring. The acacias have got their new leaves and the sugar bushes are in full blossom—like fruit trees in a miles-long orchard, some glowing rose, others gleaming white. I can think of nothing more beautiful than the view from the veranda on a morning like this. In the far distance Kilimanjaro's majestic snow-capped dome rises above the nearer Mount Meru's rounded tops, between which, cedar-covered ravines form dark shadows. To the west towers Essimingor, to the north runs the rim of the Ngorongoro crater, and beyond you can catch a glimpse of the wild mystical Oldoinyo Lengai [God's mountain], the last of the old volcanoes which still intermittently erupts. Far below us glitters the brackish Lake Manyara's metal-colored mirror, framed by thousands of pink flamingoes.

I had my coffee on the veranda and then strolled down to the garden to pick flowers, as I am expecting a guest for lunch. Udet, the German war-time flying ace, will be visiting me, and I intend to take him out for a buffalo hunt this afternoon.† He has never shot this animal and within a

---

*Jacqueline "Cockie" Birkbeck (née Alexander), Bror's second wife.
†A film crew had been in the area for some time making a film about Africa. Ernst Udet was the aviation advisor. He had been a great German flying ace in World War I, and with sixty-two kills, was second only to Richtofen, in whose squadron he flew. There is an

few days he has to return to Berlin. One of his aircraft is at the moment under repair, as one of his pilots happened to buckle its wing the other day.

The slope on the other side of the stream lies in front of me like a giant palette where the hues of hundreds of dahlias intermingle in a riot of color. The lilies you planted form a snow-white mass, and on this side, under the big greenheart trees, the cannas transform the valley into a shimmering carpet of red and gold. Metallic, gleaming honey birds flit from flower to flower, and in the fig tree grove where the spring bubbles up, the olive thrushes sing like our own nightingales.

The lawns have been newly mowed and their tender green color is spectacularly set off by a border of purple petunias. By the house itself the brick-red and darker bougainvilleas are in full bloom, and with the white madonna lilies below them providing a contrast, the whole effect is magnificent. I can only hope that everything will be as beautiful by the time you come back.

At twelve o'clock Udet arrived in the newly repaired aircraft and landed on our strip behind the house. He asked me what I thought about his homemade port wing. I had to admit I was not impressed; when the machine was resting on the ground, the wing was pointing skywards at an angle of thirty degrees. The always cheerful little German explained however that once you were airborne this was not noticeable.

For lunch I gave him fresh mushrooms, fried in butter, followed by an admirable chicken curry and rice, a dish Hassan really excels in. Juma reported that in the morning seven buffalo cows and a good bull had entered the swamp by the spring. Presumably these were the same animals I had spotted early in the morning. As they had not left the swamp by midday, they must have decided to stay there till dusk, and so there was no need for hurry, but after coffee and a short siesta we left for the Ndareda Falls at three o'clock.

The wind came from Mount Hanang, sweeping down through the valley. You remember there is a big boulder up on the crest where we thought of building. From there you have a clear view of the stream which

---

often-told story, probably apocryphal, of how in 1916 he met the French ace Guynemer in aerial combat. The confrontation lasted for eight minutes—until Udet's guns jammed. The Frenchman flew close enough to see Udet futilely hammering at his useless weapon and, with a salute and sympathetic wave, flew away. Udet survived two combat parachute jumps in the Second World War and became a high-ranking Luftwaffe officer, but eventually committed suicide.

emerges into the swamp, and in front of the boulder there is a small meadow of about twenty acres. My intention was to place Udet by the granite block and park the car on the crest by the house site in order to prevent the buffalo from crossing over here and down into the next valley. My plan was to take up the in-spoor with the four Wambulus and then slowly urge the animals towards where Udet was standing. Admittedly, he had never previously seen a buffalo, but it was not difficult to distinguish a bull from the much smaller cows. As Udet did not speak Kiswahili, it was probable that an excited native would cause more confusion than be of help, so I just gave him Cooper's* .600 Jeffrey rifle and, with a *Weidmanns heil* [a greeting roughly translating to "good hunting"], left him to go round and take up the spoors.

I soon found tracks and they were easy to follow in the soft ground. They led first over the stream and then towards dense bush. We passed a place where they had been resting and where there were some droppings, but these were cold and we continued further in.

I tested the wind—it was favorable, blowing straight towards Udet. We moved a little in the direction of Mount Hanang to be sure that the buffalo would not turn back. As we were making our flanking movement, the animals suddenly got our wind and rushed off making a lot of noise. Then everything became quiet again until they got our wind for the second time, dashing off in the direction of Udet while we stopped in expectant suspense. Then two shots were fired, reverberating between the mountains and down through the valley.

We made our way through the bush till we reached the car and then down to Udet. He had aimed at the bull and hit him, after which the

---

*Richard "Dick" Cooper was Blix's best friend and they shared some very happy times together in Africa, in Europe, and in the States. In the early 1900s, Dick's father had bought a large tract of land in Wyoming that he later disposed of, retaining the mineral rights, however. Oil was later discovered there and Dick was in line for the royalties— provided he stayed in the state for a minimum of six months a year. Dick also owned a lot of property in the United Kingdom, mostly in Yorkshire, and retained his British citizenship until his death in the early 1950s, when he drowned while duck-hunting near Singu. He was a major in the First World War, winning the MC and bar and Croix de Guerre and bar, and became a colonel while serving as military secretary to Sir Philip Mitchell in the Fiji Islands during the Second World War. Dick, who also became a friend of mine, was a great character. In order to more fully appreciate the life of luxury he led with his American friends (the Guests, the Vanderbilts, Hemingway, et cetera), Dick found it necessary to visit Africa every year in order to rough it and provide himself with a contrast.

animal had staggered, turned, and slowly cantered back into the thicker vegetation. We examined the tracks and found some blood, first by the drop but later more.

We ringed the swamp but found no spoor leading out of it. I placed Udet where the buffalo had gone in that morning and, with the natives, proceeded to follow the blood spoor. Having advanced carefully for a few hundred yards, we could hear the bull. He was obviously badly wounded and was panting heavily. I told the natives to remain behind and crawled forward in order to put him out of his misery. It was very thick there and I unfortunately happened to step on a dry twig; at the same moment the buffalo was up and away, straight towards Udet. Another shot was fired. We climbed the ridge again to be out of the way of the wounded bull in case he had turned back, and we went down to where the German was standing.

The animal had charged him but checked and went back yet another time. I now chose a spot in some comparatively open terrain on the crest of the hill for Udet and the natives to stay, and started to follow the in-spoor again. By this time the bull was understandably in a rage and there-fore dangerous. In a decisive moment like this, and in very dense bush, it is better to be alone rather than being two or more.

I found a lot of blood and followed the spoor with utmost caution and all senses alerted. It was as dense as an alder thicket at home and not a sound could be heard. Suddenly something moved some ten yards in front of me and I stopped, motionless. The smallest noise could cause flight or provoke a charge. A small tit was flitting from branch to branch—could that have been what had put the leaves in motion? It parked itself on the tip of a twig which bent under its weight and then I saw the coal-black boss of the bull's horn. The bird flew off, the twig bent back, and all was green again. But now I knew where my quarry was.

In absolute silence I shifted my position sideways inch by inch. Now I could see one ear; further back was the neck. Come along little tit. Please move the twig! But no tit would come. Then, suddenly, the bull got my wind and lifted his head a fraction.

Automatically the rifle came up to my shoulder. I could see a horn and an eye, estimated the position of the neck, and slowly squeezed the trig-ger. The heavy body collapsed—all was over.

Udet was as pleased as a schoolboy. He couldn't understand how it had all happened. A good lunch, a few minutes drive in the car, and an hour's exciting hunt. But why did the buffalo always come to exactly the place where the hunter was standing? Magic!

"I have a small Walther pistol. Keep it as a memento of this afternoon. It is the weapon I treasure most and this is the hour I've enjoyed the most in Africa."

The bull was a good specimen and the horn measured forty-eight inches and eighteen inches in circumference. We sent for people to cut up the meat and then went home. It was nice and cool on the veranda and the tea tasted fine, as did the drinks that followed.

Just as we had finished bathing and changing, Cooper arrived from Nairobi dusty and tired but pleased to be back. He was delighted to meet Udet, whom—during the four years Cooper had served as a front-line soldier in France—he had heard so much about. Udet is one of those persons who was admired by foe as well as by friend. During the course of the evening these two discussed in front of the fire all the various phases of the war—and I was all ears.

"During a certain period in 1917," Cooper said, "we were very much plagued by machine gun fire from single-seater German fighters that came over our lines at low altitude. I had sent for my heavy rifles and one day was standing with my .450 'Holland and Holland' in my hand when three aircraft came flying in. They came lower and lower and one could already hear the *rat-tat-tat* of their machine guns. They came straight at me, and I aimed well ahead of the leader. He came down like a pheasant, as did the one that followed, and I had time to reload and fire again at the third before he passed over—he also crashed. The three burnt-out planes were no more than a hundred yards from my trench." Udet asked what the aircraft looked like, and Cooper gave a description of the type.

"Yes, I remember that day very well," Udet said. "They were all three from my wing and we never got to know what had happened. You must have hit the pilots or they wouldn't have crashed so abruptly."

The room became strangely quiet. Silently they thought back to the horrible years in the mud with all the blood and stench; two brave men who had never wished each other any harm.

That night we sat up for a long time talking over our whisky and sodas. Udet told us how the repaired aircraft had got damaged. The entire film unit with its four airplanes had camped at Mtombu ("the mosquito river"). One of the younger pilots had asked to take up one of the aircraft to take a closer look at a rhino that was standing in the plain, which there was dotted with numerous sugarloaf-formed antheaps. He went up in a two-seater Klemm* and took old Ziedentopf with him. You know, the one who once owned the entire Ngorongoro crater.

When they were over the rhino, Udet observed with his field glasses how they made a dive, then up and around, followed by another dive, but this time they didn't get up.

It was only just over a mile to the spot where they had come down, so Udet started up another plane and flew over. He saw the machine lying upside down with its wheels in the air—no people could be seen but the enraged rhino was running back and forth a few hundred yards further on. Udet went down and landed close to the crashed plane. To his relief he found the two adventurers unhurt inside the machine, from which, however, they were unable to extricate themselves. He got hold of the outer edge of the rudder and managed to lift enough of the fuselage to enable them to stick out their heads, but at this stage the rhino came trotting up to see what was going on. The two incarcerated gentlemen were obliged to hastily withdraw their heads again so that Udet, who had no rifle with him, could let down the fuselage and run behind an ant heap. After a lot of snorting and stamping the rhino withdrew and Udet dared to approach a second time.

The whole procedure was then repeated. The moment Udet had grabbed hold of the rudder the rhino returned and chased him away. Having patrolled the overturned plane for some time, however, he appeared to have satisfied his curiosity and left the area. Udet saw him disappear in the distance, but was now so exhausted that he was unable to lift the machine. Luckily Ziedentopf had his sheath knife with him, and with this Udet could cut open the side of the aircraft, and so the—by now somewhat red-faced—gentlemen were liberated.

The crash had occurred when a wing had hit an antheap, and it was a miracle that no life was lost. Udet told his story in such a vivid and expressive way that his audience was actually able to see the suffering expressions on the faces of the two imprisoned persons every time the fuselage had to be let down.

Considering the bush conditions under which they had to work, it was, to say the least, a remarkable achievement for one European with the aid of two African carpenters to be able to fashion and fit a new wing and so make this plane airworthy again.

---

*The Klemm was an open-cockpit low-winged monoplane.

The moon is high and the old man up there smiles his eternal inscrutable smile. Down in the valley a couple of lions are roaring and the bull frogs are serenading, accompanied by the cicadas' finely tuned violins.

With love,
Blix

CHAPTER
2

• •

Serengeti, December

My darling Cockie,

I am sitting in my camp at Lion Hill. The big glowing ball of the sun
has disappeared behind the horizon and the plains' game are breathing
freely after the heat of the day. From the great spaces you hear the monotonous bellowing of the wildebeest; by the thousands they are slowly trekking northwards following the new tender pastures. It will soon be
Christmas and from the sportsman's point of view the plains now provide
the ideal hunting grounds. Every time I come down here to the Serengeti
I get just as impressed and enchanted as I did on my first trip by the
enormous quantity of game. The number must be limited, but nowhere
else in the world will you, within an area of this size, find such an amazing
display of wildlife.

From the top of Lion Hill you can with field glasses scan a circular area
with a diameter of sixty miles, and I don't think I am exaggerating when I
say that I have today seen a total of a million head of game, made up by
wildebeest, zebra, Grant's and Thomson's gazelle, topi, eland, and hartebeest antelopes. Do you remember the first time we came here? The grass
was burnt off and the plains were almost deserted. At that time the game
was grazing in the rainy region close to Lake Victoria and we could only
see small herds of gazelles and the odd hardy eland and hartebeest. We
had come from Ndareda over Mkalama with Ben Fourie and your friend.
Do you remember how beautiful it was at Singida, where we hunted kudu
in the stony hills and searched for the enormous buffalo with the record
head? The knotty dwarf trees twisted like windswept pines and beneath
them the wild aloes were flowering, giving the impression that entire
hillsides were on fire.

Singida is a sportsman's paradise; the small lakes abound with wild duck, there are thousands of guinea-fowl, francolin, and quail, and then the most stately of all African game, the magnificent kudu. The elephant is not particularly big here, but in this broken country with its spreading acacias and sandy river beds sparsely edged by palm trees, he harmonizes so beautifully with the terrain that you forget to think of the ivory and the revenue it may bring in.

During that safari we cleared a new route through to the Serengeti. We met the first snags some thirty miles the other side of Mkalama where a muddy stream flows into a swamp, and we had to build a bridge in order to get the lorries across. Seldom have I found so many swarms of blood-seeking mosquitos in one place. First the cook went down with malaria, then a couple of camp boys—and finally you. That time you were very ill, for more than a week you ran a temperature of over 100°, and we didn't dare to move you. Without your knowledge, I had a landing strip made in case it should prove necessary to get a doctor flown in or have you moved by air. It took a long time for you to get better and it was only when we arrived at this very spot, where I am now sitting writing, that you fully recuperated. It was a hell of a trip and I wouldn't like to have to do it again. It was mostly thanks to Fourie's untiring energy and care that we actually got through. How many times *didn't* we have to change springs and have leaking radiators soldered?

There was, however, one day I recollect with pleasure, and that was when some fifty Mkalama inhabitants arrived to fish in the swamp. They waded in line downstream towards the swamp, all the time thrusting their barbed spears into the mud. The whole operation looked pretty un-methodical, so we were somewhat surprised when they carried their catch ashore—hundreds of enormous lungfish. The biggest weighed about sixty lbs., but the natives told us that further into the swamp you could get them much bigger. They had no boats or canoes and were therefore unable to fish once they were out of their depth, but in three days they had as much dried and smoked fish as fifty men could carry. I very often think of this swamp and one day I hope to return there, bringing with me better equipment and proper fishing tackle.

Up on the hill—on the other side of the campfire—a lion has just started roaring, deeply and melodiously, and down by the Balangetti River, far from here, others are joining in. It is easy to imagine how they are arranging for a meeting and making plans for the night's hunt, at the same time announcing to everyone alive that: "Now we are the masters."

In spite of the fact that death always waits round the corner, the grass-eating animals never panic. From time to time you hear a few zebra or antelope rushing off in a wild gallop, after that neighing and calls to gather. It is the safety in numbers which keeps the wild animals calm, just as in war, when the bullets are flying, it is always easier to make larger units advance, rather than the individual.

As you know, I am now here to prepare for a big safari with an American family named Guest. They will be arriving directly from England, where they have bought a seven-seater Bellanca plane. I have engaged Raymond Hook and Ben Fourie as second hunters. I have got fifty natives with me and they are now busy building huts, preparing landing strips, et cetera. The most important things are to find the areas where the game are most numerous, the location of a few good mane lions, and above all good water. The last item is not going to be too easy, as all springs and water holes quickly got trampled up and mired by the big herds. I have with me six lorries with provisions, fuel, and tentage and intend to establish a petrol depot right here.

This morning I saw a beautiful sight. I was driving the small box-body as I arrived on the orchard-like plains on the other side of the Balangetti River when a couple of lionesses suddenly sat up in the grass, then another one, and then still more, one head after another. Finally, I counted thirty-six, and as I had a small reflex camera with me I managed to get thirty-four in one exposure. They were completely unafraid, just slightly disappointed that I had not brought any meat with me, so I had to carry on to shoot a zebra, which I towed back for them. The reaction was immediate; within a few moments all one could see was a big cloud of dust where the big cats were fighting for the goodies.

On my way back I met a lone lioness. The moment she saw me she bared her yellow fangs and her tail went up like a rocket. When I slowly approached she made a charge towards the car but stopped as soon as I gave way and disappeared in the grass, where she probably had cubs hidden away. It was nice and impressive to observe her courage and I was happy not to have to shoot. I shall have to remember to beware of her if we have to hunt in this area. Luckily, I don't think there will be much shooting on this safari—mostly photography.

Today is Monday and on Friday, I expect my party. Father Frederick, Mama Amy, the elder son Winston, the younger Raymond, and the twenty-three-year-old daughter Diana.* In addition to my two hunters I've got a European in charge of the transport and a flight mechanic. The whole operation will be somewhat unwieldy, but then we have got plenty of time. I will send you a situation report from time to time. The pilot of the plane will be Preston, who has been here before, so I know him. He is now pilot to the Duchess of Bedford ("the Flying Dutchess"), who has lent him to her American friends.

All my love,
Blix

---

*Freddie Guest was Under Secretary for Air in the British government during the First World War. His wife Amy sponsored Amelia Earhart's successful attempt in 1928 to be the first woman to fly the Atlantic. Winston Guest was a ten-goal polo player, and Raymond—a former United States ambassador to Ireland—was also a high-handicap international polo player. The family were clients of Blix's on many subsequent occasions.

· ·

Serengeti

Dear Dick,

Yesterday I was out all night. I drove out early in the morning, which left me all day for a thorough survey of water resources, land features, and of course the quantity and species of wild animals in the area. The majority of the game seems to concentrate here in the vicinity of Lion Hill, and if we get one or two additional heavy showers the chances are that they will stay put.

I also found plenty of game by the hills, west of the plains, and here I counted at least fifteen lions. You may remember that there is a small spring with clear fresh water situated between two cliff faces. I left the car and started climbing up to it when I heard a deep growl, giving fair warning. Although the rifle automatically came up to my shoulder, I had no intention of firing, unless I was forced to. I stood motionless for a few moments, trying to spot the animal, but everything was quiet and calm. I took a few cautious steps forward and at the same moment a big lion with a magnificent black mane stood up. He was nervously lashing his muscular sides with his tail, the fangs were bared, and above them the cruel yellow eyes were watching me, politely asking me to: "Go to hell." As soon as I conformed with his wish he became quiet again. I should think he probably had a kill by the spring and wanted to finish his meal in peace, before retiring for his siesta. However, we shall meet again, old-timer!

I went through the pass, down towards Lake Victoria. On the way I saw a couple of very good impalas and some ten roan antelopes. A big leopard was sunning himself in a flat-topped thorn tree and half hidden in the grass below was his wife. When I got nearer they hurried off in long graceful leaps, but I hope to get the opportunity of renewing the acquaintance.

It was exceptionally beautiful there, and the plains looked like an orchard in flower with the tender bright green of the foliage and the new grass providing a contrast. The landscape looked like an enormous park and made me think of pictures of nineteenth-century hunting scenes. Towards the end of the valley, down by the narrow riverbed, I found some recent buffalo tracks and therefore decided to stay the night in the vicinity in the hope of getting to see them either that evening or next morning.

I had two cars with me, as I did not want to run the risk of the same thing happening to me that did last time I was here. That time I had taken out a British lady and had only one vehicle. We happened to break a back axle when we were nearly fifty miles from camp and we were not rescued for another week. I couldn't let her walk the distance, nor could I leave her alone with two natives with whom she was unable to communicate and who also refused to walk through the lion-infested country.

I chose a concealed spot for my simple camp and here I left two natives while Juma and myself continued down to the riverbed. As you may remember it is open grassland on both sides with only a few acacias with enormous crowns growing here and there. The game appeared to be undisturbed. Five buffalo bulls were grazing by themselves, and in the distance I could through the field glasses see some twenty animals. There didn't seem to be any need for further scouting, so I drove back. It was now past five o'clock and the shadows were growing longer.

The chattering monkeys were jumping about in the stunted trees along the river, looking for wild fruit and leaf buds for their evening meal. The brief hour of tropical twilight is pleasant and fascinating; this is when everything comes alive after the oppressive heat of the day, and it really can become very hot, as we are only 3,500 feet above sea level. This particular place cannot be called a health resort, but then there should be no need to move from the main camp for more than a day or so at a time.

I didn't see any buffalo higher upstream, but there were plenty of tracks. There were three cheetahs lying on an antheap enjoying the last rays of sun. I managed to cross the valley without being seen and could then steal up to them to within a range of ten yards, from where I could photograph them.

During the night I could hear lions all around me, both far off and nearby, and very close to the camp two leopards were making their peculiar coughing sound. The harsh voice of the arch enemy immediately woke up a troop of baboons that already had settled in for the night and the stillness was shattered by their wild war cries. I had no great difficulty in interpreting this fearful noise and putting it into human language.

Early this morning I returned to the main camp and it was rather like going through Noah's ark. It is almost impossible to describe the enormous quantity of game you see—just one vast mass of wildebeest, zebra, antelope, and gazelle.

Farah has demarcated the landing strip and put up a wind sock. He has also prepared two runways by towing flat-topped thorn trees, doing the work of big brooms, back and forth. It was fortunate he had started this work at once, as Manley of African Guides* had sent down a Wilson Airways plane with important telegrams and letters. The pilot was Tom Black† and he had had no trouble in spotting the landing strip, as Farah had lit a smoke fire as soon as he had heard the engine noise from the aircraft.

The camp staff had had some difficulties in keeping the runways free from game, and Tom was obliged to make a few nose dives to scare the animals off before he dared to land.

He informed me that my party would arrive according to schedule and the transport with the extra staff, white hunters, and provisions would be here the following day. He also gave me two telegrams inquiring whether I would be able to take on two new safaris immediately after this one; one was for two young Americans from Chicago, Jack Simpson (the polo player) and Armour (from the meat-canning family), the other one for Alfred Vanderbilt.

It was pleasant to get a chat with Tom. He is always bright and cheerful and over a whisky and soda we revived old memories. We particularly relived an occasion when, in a Gipsy Moth, we had failed on takeoff to gain sufficient height to clear a thin forest belt and had to weave our way between the trees until we could finally climb. Those were very exciting moments.

I have arranged the camp in such a way that the sleeping tents, with their doorways pointing outwards, are sited in a semicircle round the common campfire. Behind them is the mess tent, and behind this again

---

*Blix's safari company, which he co-owned with Philip Percival.
†Tom Campbell Black was a pioneer aviator in East Africa and winner of the 1934 England–Australia race. He was Beryl Markham's flying instructor and probably her only true love.

the cook has established his kitchen. I have marked out a special parking place for the Bellanca plane and the trucks. This will be under the supervision of Ben Fourie, who also has his tent here. We shall be staying here for approximately ten days and using this camp as a base. I intend to make minor daily trips with one or more safari guests at a time.

This afternoon I drove out westwards, and although there wasn't much game about I saw plenty of lions. Most of them were sunning themselves on the cliffs, and they were watching the movement of the cars with interest as we drove past. I shot a few zebras for them and dragged the bodies up to the cliffs. One of the zebras, however, got wounded and I rushed around some outcrops to finish it off, but three lions were quicker and killed it less than two hundred yards from where I was watching.

Later in the afternoon, I was wandering around by myself in a small riverbed, overshadowed by yellow thorn trees and edged by dense stiff grass and fleshy-leafed vegetation. Suddenly I heard a low, angry hissing sound. I stopped at once with the rifle raised. Again a jungle dweller politely but firmly requesting me to take another way. What kind of creature could it be this time? The sound had come from the base of a tree some twenty yards away, but I couldn't see anything there. Presently, a blade of grass slowly moved and beneath it I could now see a narrow vibrating tongue. Again the hissing could be heard and immediately afterwards the head and expanded neck of a cobra rose from the grass. Why shoot? It had given me an honest warning and asked me to leave, and when I slowly withdrew, it made itself invisible again, satisfied and reassured. One so very seldom sees a snake, but if it occasionally happens on safari, the native hunter always considers it as a good omen. During my twenty-five years of wandering in the African bush, neither I nor any of my staff have ever been bitten by a snake; they are shy creatures and generally crawl away whenever they meet a human being. The native has got very good eyesight and if you have one walking in front of you it is fairly certain that you won't be unpleasantly caught out by a poisonous reptile.

I shall be very busy for some time and there will be no time for writing, but when the safari is over I'll send you a résumé of what's happened and my plans for the near future.

Regards,
Blix

CHAPTER
3

Nairobi, December

My dear Dick,

The first part of this safari is now finished and we are in Nairobi after ten perfect days on the Serengeti. It is easy to please anybody down there as our creator has blessed the area with so many interesting sights that it is almost unbelievable. Apart from this we have also been lucky and the weather has been fine all the time. We have had no trouble with the transport and the plane has performed a shuttle service between the camp and Nairobi, taking the girl to the hairdresser and the boys to a ball at Government House, et cetera.

Winston, who was out with Raymond Hook, shot the big lion by the spring and Father Freddie got a good leopard, probably the one I saw in the tree the day I drove towards Lake Victoria. It would have amused you to have been there with us, since this was not far from the place where you wounded the lion that then charged you and you shot when he was almost on top of you.

The leopard was lying out in the open, enjoying the early morning sunshine, but as soon as it caught sight of us he moved off in long graceful leaps and disappeared into the nearest bushes. He was out of range for shooting, so we sat down to wait until he had quieted down and chosen his sleeping quarters for the day.

An hour later we circled the thicket and discovered that he had followed a sandy riverbed upstream. We then made a detour so as not to scare him, before again approaching the riverbed. Now we could not find any tracks and he must therefore have been somewhere between us and the point where we had left the spoor. A bit further down a ravine opened out into the riverbed and here I positioned Freddie and myself. I then sent Juma and two of the porters back along the detour with orders to restart the tracking and to proceed slowly, whistling softly. In this way they would drive the leopard towards us. As soon as they heard shots fired they were to run out into the open, since a wounded leopard in dense bush is an awkward and dangerous customer to deal with.

After half an hour we could hear the first low whistles in the distance, and a bit later a twig snapped, making only a faint crack. Something must be approaching. Freddie was ready with the camera and I stood by his side, prepared to hand him his rifle. A couple of minutes passed in complete silence. One could hear one's own heart beating and the blood was pulsating at a faster rate than usual.

Emerging from the dark shadows of the dense undergrowth the outline of a golden-spotted form came gliding slowly. You could plainly see the perfect movement of the muscles under the velvety skin, but the soft sand deadened any sound from the great paws.

The camera was raised to the eye and a faint *click* was heard. The leopard stopped for a fraction of a second but then, unconcernedly, continued on his way. The camera was quickly exchanged for the rifle, a shot was fired, and the big yellow cat collapsed as if struck by lightning—never to move again. It was a good shot, a little high in the shoulder, but instantaneously fatal.

The natives were called in, everybody registering pride and pleasure. They had all done well and old Freddie was delighted, mostly because he had managed to get such a good photo. On another day, however, we were not so successful. Early in the morning Raymond and I had been out and seen a magnificent lion slinking off into a bush-covered valley. Raymond wanted to go after him at once, but I told him it would be better to wait until the sun had risen higher and one could be certain of the place the lion had chosen for his midday rest. He could then position himself higher up in the valley and have the lion driven straight towards him and so get a good chance at a shot.

At eleven o'clock we left camp together with Father Freddie and daughter Diana, who both insisted on coming. Having arrived at the starting point, I chose an antheap, big as a house, as their observation post. This was situated in the middle of a park landscape made up by big yellow thorn trees just where the thickets of the valley emerged into open country.

"Now stand here, all three of you, and remain quiet as mice, and most important, don't move. Remember, it is Raymond who is going to shoot.

It is his lion, he saw it first, and it is for him all this has been arranged. You other two are merely spectators!"

The undergrowth where the lion had gone to look for his resting place was thick and thorny. I had only two natives with me. They were not carrying spears and to have sent in two unarmed men against a lion who certainly would become angered and possibly wounded would not have been fair, so I went in with them myself.

We crept forward slowly through the bush—every now and then sounding low whistles or muted "shooh-shoohs." Five minutes passed and then suddenly came a deep, throaty roar. There he was! Everything became quiet again and we continued cautiously with mounting tension. Then a shot was fired, then another one and yet another, and finally a whole fusillade. What the hell was going on? After all, they had no automatic weapons with them! I called the two natives and we ran as fast as we could out into the open. A wounded lion is the most dangerous creature there is.

We arrived at the antheap.

"Hallo there, what's happened?"

Diana was sitting in the top of the tree nearest the antheap, Raymond was on a branch a little lower down, and old Freddie was still climbing.

"What on earth is going on?"

"You said *one* big lion. Instead, thirty-eight came out, big ones as well as small. We climbed this tree as fast as we could and started firing in the air to frighten them off."

"But for God's sake," I asked in despair, "what happened to the one with the black mane?"

"He ran away whilst we were climbing!"

Well, that was that. The fault was of course entirely mine; I should have relied more on the unarmed beaters rather than an inexperienced newcomer. However, it had been an exciting day for us all, even if the three safari members, during the few moments of commotion, had been unable to fully appreciate the impressive sight of thirty-eight lions galloping along. Still, no animal got wounded, no person came to any harm, and there are lots of other lions. Better luck next time!

One morning I drove the two young men down to the place where I had first seen the buffalo. There was plenty of game all along the route and the men were taking photographs most of the time. We also got the opportunity to feed several lions. One of them came up close to us and trotted beside the car, looking for meat. We had shot a Thomson's gazelle for our own dinner, and I asked Juma, who was sitting in the back, to cut off a leg and hand it to me. I held it outside the car and the lion immediately came up and graciously took it from my hand.

These big cats are becoming too tame, and accidents could well happen if one of them should get too close to an inexperienced person who became nervous or acted carelessly. The other night, a couple of days before my party arrived, I had seen something moving in the camp and looked out of my tent door. Three lions were standing in the moonlight drinking out of my bathtub. If a newcomer—just having left civilization and brought up on horror tales and distorted nursery stories about the king of beasts—had panicked, shouted, run away, or fired, the lion would probably, instinctively and purely for reasons of self-preservation, have charged him and torn him to pieces.

We arrived in "the buffalo country" at about ten o'clock, and fresh tracks and droppings showed that the animals had been grazing there during the night and early hours of the morning. We left the cars in an open space surrounded by bush, and asked the staff to put up tents, collect water and firewood, and prepare food.

We ourselves, with Juma and two gunbearers, proceeded down the valley to reconnoiter. From the multitude of tracks it was possible to determine where a lone bull could be found; three other bulls had been walking by themselves. Further over some twenty animals had been grazing and then crossed over to the other side of the valley. While we were looking, a big herd of giraffe constantly kept in front of us. Sometimes they stood still, watching us with their big gentle eyes, sometimes they set off in their peculiar slow-motion gallop. This was very annoying, as they would now probably warn the wary buffalo about our presence.

About three miles further down we got a clear view of both sides, and here we caught sight of five buffalo standing in the shade of a big acacia five hundred yards away from us. The wind was in our favor and, following the riverbed, we managed to get up to within a hundred and fifty yards of them. We stopped and examined them through our field glasses. They were all old bulls, but two were better than the others. We now agreed that Winston should take the bull to the right and Raymond the one to the left. In case the others, after the firing, should come down towards us, Winston was to shoot the first animal and Raymond the last; this to avoid them aiming at the same target.

We didn't hurry and when the boys were ready I counted to three; two shots were fired almost simultaneously. Winston's bull fell immediately, Raymond's indicated a probable heart shot, and the four galloped slowly towards the sheltering bushes.

"Take the other one, I'll take care of the wounded one!"

Raymond fired and the bull went down. Winston missed. Just as I was going to fire at the wounded bull before he disappeared into the thicket, he also went down.

Three good bulls within a few minutes—a successful hunt. The gun-bearers complimented us and shook hands in the usual manner, and the youngest went back to fetch one car and tell the driver of the other to go back to camp and return with a truck, skinners, and salt for the hides. There was going to be some feasting for all of us. Buffalo meat is delicious, and the thought of roasted marrow bones made my mouth water.

Having photographed the carcasses and measured the heads we wandered back for lunch and a siesta. The truck arrived at three o'clock, and after I had instructed the natives how to deal with the meat, hides, and horns, we returned to the main camp.

That same day Raymond Hook had been out with Freddie, Amy, and Diana. They had got some excellent photographs and Diana had shot a good lion right on Lion Hill, just above our camp.

The plane had gone up to Nairobi and returned with mail, fresh vegetables, fruit, and butter. We had a jolly evening celebrating with champagne with our dinner, then gramophone music and native dancing.

One day I was out with Mrs. Guest and Diana, partly to take photographs and partly to try and get a lion for Amy, all the others having got theirs. We had been bumping along on the plains most of the day and one *donga* [a pit or depression in the plain, often with very steep walls, filled with tall grass and thorn trees and used as cover by animals] after one another had been "beaten." Late in the afternoon, when it was almost dark, we at last saw a good black-maned lion lying in the grass in front of the dense thicket. We drove round in a wide circle, left the car behind some cliffs, and crept forward in the grass, seeking cover behind trees and bushes. We managed to get within eighty yards of him, which was as far as the open terrain would permit. I instructed Mrs. Guest on how to aim, myself standing prepared with my double-barreled rifle. Then I softly whistled. The lion rose leisurely and looked around. He was a magnificent sight where he stood; proud, composed, and unafraid.

The bullet hit, but too far behind the shoulder, and with a roar he disappeared into the bushes. This was not so good; the sun was about to go down and to leave him there till next day would probably mean that he would stiffen up, be at the mercy of the hyenas, and there would be nothing left of him.

We went back to the car and slowly drove round the thicket. A few roars told us that he was far from dead, so I told the ladies to remain in the car while I went to take a closer look at him.

You know yourself what such a situation is like and how suddenly a charge can be expected. It is always just as dangerous but equally as exciting. I chose the thinnest opening in the bush and crept cautiously forward step by step. Nothing happened: everything was nerve-wrackingly silent. Then I suddenly got a glimpse of a yellow form gliding through the shadows and fired immediately. I heard the bullet hit, but no sound came from the lion. I knew he wouldn't be easy to deal with. I was now pretty keyed up and it felt as if my Adam's apple had been replaced by a big lump of cotton wool, which I had great difficulties in swallowing, but I had to go on. Inch by inch I crept forward, with every muscle tensed for instant action.

I saw something black peeping out of the grass—a lion's ear. I stretched myself and could now see the whole head. He was dead. But what was this—he had a yellow mane and the animal we had seen and shot at a few minutes ago was black-maned. Then I understood. I had shot another lion, and the relief I had just felt vanished as quickly as it had overtaken me. The wounded lion must be very close, and the next moment I heard a tremendous roar immediately to my right and out of the bushes rushed the black-maned lion—not towards me, but towards the car! He stopped for a short moment, furiously lashing his flanks with his tail, whilst a dull roar, full of hatred, rumbled in his throat.

Everything now happened very quickly. The danger for those in the car was imminent; I leapt to one side to get a clear line of fire and the next moment he charged like a rocket straight towards the vehicle. I got him high in the shoulder, and he rolled around like a hare.

My nerves certainly were a bit frayed, and when I had time to think of what could have happened if the bullet had not hit the right place, my knees became a bit wobbly. I don't believe the ladies would even have had time to realize what an efficient killer the lion is.

After a bit of trouble we managed to get the lions into the car, and there was great jubilation when we arrived back in camp. Raymond Hook was the only one who fully realized, when I related the sequence of events to him, how very generous the good God had been.

Yours ever,
Blix

. . . .

My dear Dick,

I am now in Nairobi with my "family" and there are lots of things to see to—film has to be developed, heads mounted, hides cured, hotels and bars visited, and friends called upon ad infinitum. While all this is going on the camp will be moved to Mbulu Escarpment, where I already have selected a suitable site, and tomorrow Preston will fly me there. The group will stay on here for another couple of days and is living at Muthaiga Club, where they appear to get on well and have already made many friends in Nairobi. Tonight there is a big dance at Torr's Hotel—and you know what that implies. They are all in high spirits, and pleased with what they've seen.

I intend to stay at Mbulu for a week. There are some good rhino there and big buffalo. In addition, the scenery is beautiful and the climate very healthy. I have been to see your friend Chief Michaele and asked him to send out scouts to locate the three big rhinos I know are there. He has also promised to find me some Wadikidiki hunters. They are very strange people—a very small clan, with only some hundred members remaining from a tribe of pygmies that have dwelled in this area for a thousand years or more. They are a bit taller than the Wambutis of the Congo and darker in color, but then they are not like them—forest people—but live in open country and more exposed to the sun. Like all pygmies they are wary and do not mix easily with other tribes.

After Mbulu we may move to Singida for kudu and some bird shooting, but no definite plans have as yet been made. On the subject of Singida, Mkalama, and pygmies, one has in this area found rock carvings executed by the bushmen—some of them very beautiful.

The Wambulus are a tribe of relatively recently immigrating Hamites, probably an offshoot of the Watutsi. They moved south during the great displacement of tribes hundreds of years ago. Some time ago I read in an American travel book describing these parts that I was the only white man who had made any contact with the Wadikidiki. My knowledge of them, however, does not go any further than having gained some part of their confidence and their willingness to go hunting with me. Their own form of hunting is to have the game driven. A few hunters lie in ambush with bows and arrows, whilst others drive the wild animals towards them. In this area I have seen other natives from different tribes using the same method. Such was the case when I observed a bunch of Wanderobos from the Kenya–Tanganyika border, hunting on the Serengeti Plains. On a slight rise in the ground they had constructed a dozen cairns, and behind these a number of men had taken cover. A herd of zebra and wildebeest were grazing in the valley down below, and the wind was coming from their direction, blowing towards the concealed hunters. I had positioned myself with my field glasses on top of a small hill some distance away and was very much looking forward to the development of events. From a distance of about a mile one could see a number of hunters, armed with bows and arrows, advancing towards the game in a sort of easy lope. As the animals were grazing in the bottom of the valley, they were unable to get the scent of the approaching hunters.

At a distance of about two hundred yards the hunters broke into a sprint and, shouting wildly, they rushed towards the zebras and antelopes. These were seized by panic and careered off in a cloud of dust straight towards the concealed men. I imagined then that I could see the logic of the plan; this way of hunting would follow the usual pattern. I was therefore taken by surprise when I saw the intended marksmen suddenly leaving their hideouts shouting like demons. The panic-stricken and confused animals stopped for a moment in hesitation, then turned about and ran straight into the line of men who now, hidden by the clouds of dust, were just in front of them. They were able to discharge their arrows from a range of ten yards, bagging ten zebras as a reward for their pains.

It was a cunning plan and well thought out (to let the quarry produce its own "smoke screen" behind which the hunters approach unseen), and the results were impressive.

So, I'll be leaving tomorrow. We have been shopping all day, and Nairobi is a tempting town for the sportsman. For African conditions I think Chas A. Heyer has as good a selection of guns and rifles as you could possibly wish for. This is important, particularly when you are out with Americans, as the weaponry they bring out with them, and which they use in the Rocky Mountains and in Alaska, does not carry the high velocity which is required for the big game here. The male members of the party have now got .350 Rigbys and .450 Holland and Holland Mark IIs, and they can be used for everything. The ladies have each brought a 7mm Mauser and, in addition, a Paradox.* They have also brought out cameras of all sizes and models, I believe a total of some twenty.

It looks as if they are quite impressed with Nairobi, and thanks to their letters of introduction they have had the opportunity of meeting many pleasant people and have been invited for lunch to Government House.

The town is teeming with friends from the Highlands and the surrounding country. It will soon be Christmas, and they are all here for the shopping and to enjoy themselves. Muthaiga Club and the hotels are fully booked, there is dancing every night, and the champagne is flowing.

Yours ever,
Blix

---

*A shotgun with the business end three inches of the barrel rifled. Usually loaded with ball in the right barrel and SSG shot in the left, it's the ideal defense weapon against a charging lion or leopard.

CHAPTER

4

Dearest Cockie,

We had an uncomfortable flight down with lots of squalls and air pockets. It is always very turbulent over Lake Magadi and on one occasion we were shot up five hundred feet in a flash. It was an unpleasant sensation and I was only waiting for an equally speedy descent. Over the Escarpment the ceiling was very low and we doubted if we would be able to find our runway. However, on the other side of the ridge the weather was clear and, thanks to Farah's smoke fires, which were visible for a considerable distance, we were able to land without mishap.

Two of the staff were ill, so I sent them back with the plane to Nairobi Hospital. Now I've got two days at my disposal to locate the various animals, arrange for porters, et cetera. I don't believe I'll have any difficulties, as Chief Michaele himself is here and has with him numerous scouts and guides. Ever since I was here with the Prince of Wales—when the chief received the King's Medal—he has proved himself a good and helpful friend. From a personal point of view, I like him very much indeed and also respect his people, the Wambulus. One of their most important moral commandments is the same as ours, "Thou shall not steal," and this is a fairly rare kind of morality in East Africa. During all the years I have lived in this area it has never happened that anything has been stolen from me by the natives, and if by chance something should have fallen off a car or disappeared in some other way it has always, if found, been returned to the owner. It is a handsome tribe. The men are tall, well made, and upright, and the women are real beauties—what more can you expect from the back of beyond? This last phrase, I now feel, is entirely misconceived, because where else in the world could you find a more beautiful countryside? Below us the Rift Valley stretches out in a wide sweep, framed by an imposing range of mountains and fertile highlands. In the distance, the snow-capped dome of Kilimanjaro is raised against the sky, and on either side of the Escarpment the Manyara and Eyasi lakes compete in idyllic beauty and display of white, red, and blue (soda, flamingoes, and water) color. Let us imagine a Mbulu visiting London. I feel sure he would not feel content until he again picked his way along the winding paths of the Escarpment, again beheld the familiar square earthen huts, and again heard the tinkle from the bells of the leading herd animals in the hills—home again from London, and what he would consider "the back of beyond."

I have been out with your old friend, Saleh the skinner, whom I had sent out to look for kudu. Yesterday he came back with the good news that he had seen a fine bongo bull on a mountain slope not far from here. As you know, no bongo has ever been shot in Tanganyika. I once told the game warden in Dar-es-Salaam that I had seen spoors from bongo in the bamboo forest beyond Ngorongoro, but I was put off with a shrug.

I went with Saleh to the place where he had seen the bull, and examined the spoor. There was no doubt. Later I showed Michaele a photo of a bongo head from *Rowland Ward's Records of Big Game*, and he in his turn showed it to his own hunters and to the Wadikidiki, who were all unanimous in their opinion that the bongo lived in the area but was extremely wary, which we of course already knew. One day I intend to return here by myself with a few Wanderobos and their dogs—and then the game warden will be provided with proof!

There is plenty of buffalo here and several rhinos. So far, there have been no reports of kudu, but Michaele's scouts have informed us that there are quite a few at Ndareda. The three big rhinos I know are here have as yet not been tracked down.

Our landing strip is fine—one thousand yards long—but runs only in one direction, east-west. Should the wind come from the wrong direction it will be necessary to land at Cooper's farm, twenty miles from here, and then do this bit by car. The road is pretty bad but passable.

All my love,
Blix

My darling Cockie,

My American friends arrived yesterday at eleven o'clock, a bit tired after the hectic days in town and pleased to be back in camp again. Cooper is with them. In the afternoon we amused ourselves by shooting guinea-fowl and quail, which generally come in on our runway, and of these we got some twenty-five brace, so had a delicious supper.

The evening could have ended in disaster. At five o'clock Dick Cooper decided to fly with Preston over the Ngorongoro crater, where he hadn't been since he'd hunted there with me several years ago. It was admittedly somewhat late in the day to undertake such a project, but they said they would only fly round for a short while and come straight back. At the last moment Freddie and the younger son decided to go with them, and so they set off.

I myself took a bath, shaved, and tidied up the camp after the move that day. Two trucks with provisions and equipment had also arrived from Nairobi and the unloading had to be supervised.

I could not rid myself of an uneasy feeling about this flight. Preston was unfamiliar with the flying conditions over the crater and Dick had not been there for a long time; it was also late in the day and our landing strip was not easy to find, hidden as it was in thick bush country. I arranged for the smoke fires and all available hurricane lamps to be lit and had spare fuel brought out to the runway.

The sun went down behind the mountains, and I imagined that the twilight came sooner than usual. There is absolutely nowhere one can make a forced landing between Ngorongoro and the camp. I was soon pacing up and down, all the time listening and hoping for the sound of an engine.

In no time it was almost completely dark and still nothing could be heard. I gathered all available personnel and the hurricane lamps were placed twelve on each side of the runway. The smoke fires were stoked up and the flames were soon rising high. The headlamps from the vehicles illuminated the entire runway. All light had gone when at last I heard a faint engine noise far away. It grew louder and then we could see the aircraft making a circle around the runway before landing.

Our friends climbed out, Cooper and Preston a bit pale beneath their suntan. Preston calmly said, "Thank you, Blix," and Cooper croaked, "You saved our lives." Those two were the only ones who fully understood what the consequences would have been had they failed to see our signals.

They had of course stayed too long over the crater, fascinated by the quantity of game down there, and failed to take into account that they would have to contend with the down draft when again climbing to seven thousand feet in order to clear the crater rim. Having at last managed to gain sufficient altitude, they were unable to see our landing lights, and Preston had already told Cooper that he intended to risk a forced landing when Dick replied, "Just five minutes more, please, I know Blix will signal us." A minute later, they spotted the flickering flames from our fires.

It is impossible to describe the anxiety one feels in moments like these and equally difficult to explain the relief, once it's all happily over.

We sat up late that evening around the campfire under the starlit sky. We made plans for the following day and retold stories about adventures and hunts in days gone by.

The merry fire was warming and the sparkling whiskies and sodas were refreshing. The gramophone and radio got competition from frogs and crickets, occasionally interrupted by howls from the hyenas and the prolonged shrieks from barn owls. Further down the valley, the lions were calling each other for their nightly meetings.

The following morning I went out with Freddie after rhino; Raymond Hook took out Winston; and Ben Fourie and Dick accompanied Diana. Chief Michaele had placed hunters and trackers at our disposal, and, with three Wadikidikis, came along with me and Freddie. We took a luncheon basket with us containing food, lime juice, a few bottles of soda water, and some gin. One of the natives carried the medicine bag with bandages, iodine, morphia, Pasteur's snake serum, et cetera.

We first went to a salt lick in a small overgrown glen to see if there were any fresh tracks there, but it proved not to have been visited during the night. The engine noises and the general hullabaloo from the camp had probably scared them off. A bit later, however, we came upon fresh tracks of a cow rhino. We followed these in the hope that they would join up with others. They led through dense clumps of vegetation, where she had fed on thorn bushes and aloes, and there she had also been feasting on a great favorite, the young shoots of the euphorbia tree. These look rather like pin cushions and are as prickly, so I don't imagine added spices would be required to stimulate the appetite.

Eventually the tracks brought us to a waterhole where she had enjoyed a mudbath and where other rhinos also had been rooting about. We found the big imprints of a bull and the smaller ones of what probably was a cow. We followed the former and within half an hour came up to the bull, who was standing in a patch of thorn scrub, peacefully munching away and enjoying the early morning sunshine.

His horn was not up to much, and as we had decided not to shoot at anything less than twenty-five inches, we confined our activities to taking photos and got some excellent shots both with the Contex and with color film.

We went back a short distance, stopped, and sent out scouts in different directions. In the meantime, we made a small fire, brewed tea, and rested. After about an hour the scouts returned. Two of them had seen a very good rhino, two miles farther on, and the rest had found fresh buffalo spoor in a meadow a mile further down the valley. We decided to first follow the rhino with our trackers and gunbearers; the rest of the natives were instructed to locate the buffalo, and we were all to meet at midday beneath an easily spotted landmark, a cliff about a mile away from our resting place.

We found the rhino close to the place where he had been seen by the scouts, but he was standing in thick bush which was difficult to penetrate. We glimpsed the slate-gray back, and when he from time to time raised his head we could see the long pointed horn. In that kind of bushy terrain it was impossible to get near the animal without giving away one's presence, and so we made a detour to reach a waterhole nearby. It was almost certain that the rhino was on his way there to drink before retiring to his lair for the day. Having reached the waterhole, we sat down to wait, well concealed by thick bush and with the wind blowing towards us. We didn't know if we had guessed right, so it was all fairly exciting. We thought we had an hour's wait in front of us, but in much less than that we heard twigs being broken in the thickets. The tick-birds* that generally attach themselves to the beasts' backs and sides in search of parasites were emitting their usual shrill chattering calls whenever leaves and small twigs brushed against them, and we knew that a big one was coming.

After about a quarter of an hour he appeared and stood for a while by the side of the waterhole, peering at the sun, unbelievably ugly, grotesque, unreal—a live tank from the wilds.

The horn was a good one and I estimated it would measure twenty-four inches in length. We agreed that our first aim should be to obtain some good photos. The rhino's eyesight is extremely poor at distances over fifty yards and his hearing is not all that good either, but his ally and attendant the tick-bird was now, as so many times in the past, going to upset our plans. By shrill screeches and flapping of wings they informed their hosts that there was danger afoot, and the beast started to walk irritably back and forth. The cameras were put away again and we crept forward with our heavy rifles. When we were about fifty yards away he appeared to make up his mind about from where the danger threatened, and with his head raised he trotted slowly in our direction.

I had advised Freddie that if presented with a frontal shot against this particular beast he should aim at the point of shoulder, past the head, and, just as the bull broke into a gallop, he fired and hit him at exactly the right spot. A few convulsive movements of the heavy head—and all was over.

It was now eleven o'clock. We measured the horn and found it was a little more than twenty-five inches. I sent word to camp for more people to help with the usual chores—skinning, cutting up the meat, et cetera—and dispatched a message to the cliff calling back the scouts we had left there.

In the shadow of a big acacia we prepared a place to rest during the hottest hours of the day and put up the table and safari chairs we had brought with us. Siphons, lime juice, and gin were unpacked, and with the help of ice from a thermos we mixed ourselves some refreshing drinks with which we saluted each other in the picturesque surroundings. Hav-

---

*The tick-bird referred to is the red-billed ox-pecker.

ing lunched on guinea-fowl with curry and rice, pineapple, and strong coffee we dozed off—far away from all worries, the tiny camp fidgets, and women's perpetual inquiries!

All my love,
Blix

Mbulu

My darling Cockie,

Since I last wrote you I've been on four days' safari with the two brothers, and I will now try to give you an account of our experiences.

As you've been to Mbulu you will remember the white fort built by the Germans during the great world war in that old-fashioned fortress style which we recall from the story books of our childhood: built around a courtyard, with a well in the middle, crenellated turrets, a moat and drawbridge. This is where the district commissioner resides and this is where we went to call on him. After that we went to Michaele's house, where the chief's trackers awaited us. They were the same men I had employed when I had hunted in this vicinity with the Prince of Wales and we had seen the tracks of the two rhinos we now intended to look for. Michaele insisted that these animals were still in the area; one had a bent toenail, the other left a spoor as if he had a stiff leg. The natives told us that the two bulls usually kept to their own limited habitats, separated from each other by some six miles, and we decided to explore the nearest one first.

He lived in the great forest just behind the White Father's Mission, and we put up our first camp fairly close to the mission buildings. We called on my old friends there, and the bearded Catholic monks were as hospitable and friendly as always. They look after their stomachs and their gardens with equal care and attention, and after a pleasant chat these jovial Frenchmen presented us with beautiful fresh vegetables and eggs. As Michaele is a follower of the Protestant faith, there are often differences of opinion, within the religious field, between him and the mission, and the poor Wambulus consequently get many confusing problems to sort out.

We put up our tents at the edge of the forest, well protected from the wind. The vegetation there mostly consisted of wild olive interspersed with solitary giant podocarpus trees. A stream murmured in the valley below the hill, and behind the camp there was a spring, discharging its waters down the mountainside in a gently curving pattern.

It was cold up there, six thousand five hundred feet above sea level, and the campfire was prepared, bigger than usual.

A bushbuck was barking in the undergrowth, and in the dim interior of the forest the vervet monkeys and colobus were quarreling about the best quarters for the night. The dry cough of a leopard could be heard down in the riverbed and another one was answering quite close to the camp. The air was filled with the eternal chirps of the crickets, and above the dark treetops the stars twinkled in the clear night. Someone put more wood on the fire.

At an unmercifully early hour the next morning Juma arrived with the usual steaming cup of tea, meaning it was time to get up. The trackers were already huddled round the fire with their blankets well drawn up over their heads and shoulders and the gunbearers were busy with cleaning rods and pull-throughs. The cook was putting the last provisions in the luncheon basket, and after a quick breakfast of bacon and eggs and a cup of coffee we were ready to set off. There was just enough light for tracking and it was bitterly cold. The thermometer showed plus four centigrade and the knee-high grass was white with heavy dew. We followed one of the numerous rhino paths that crisscrossed the forest. The gradient of the path, in this type of broken country, was extremely well laid out, as if it had been surveyed and made with the aid of every kind of modern instrument. The rhinoceros, and perhaps even more so the elephant, is nature's master roadbuilder.

After an hour's march we found fresh night-tracks from a cow and half-grown calf. As they seemed to lead in the same direction we intended to take, we followed them. Numerous piles of droppings on either side of the path indicated that there were plenty of rhino about. Having walked on for yet another hour we came to a swamp. By then the sun was up, but the shadows were still deep and white clouds of mist were clinging to the moist ground. Out in the mire the cow and her calf were standing covered with mud after their morning bath, obviously waiting for the sun to dry and harden the clay on their back until it became an effective shield against parasites.

At the edge of the swamp we found the fresh spoor of several buffalo, but just then we had more pressing interests. We left the path and made a detour with the wind behind us so as not to unnecessarily disturb mother and child. Having walked for a mile or so the tracker in front suddenly stopped as if petrified and pointed to the ground. There in front of us was a clear imprint of a rhino's near fore—with a broken toenail. One of "my" animals.

It is difficult to explain to somebody who hasn't been there the thrill one feels in a moment like that.

The first round was ours; we had found the right spoor, at the right place and right time. Now, however, all the uncertainties lay ahead, and so much could happen: the wind could change; a bird could give us away; perhaps the buffalo, whose tracks we'd seen, were between us and the old one; even the monkeys spoke a language he was well able to interpret.

Judging from the dew on the ground he had passed there sometime after midnight and his spoor was easy to follow. We continued silently and cautiously and soon came upon some scattered dung. The droppings were fresh but cold, so we could proceed somewhat faster. Presently, we got out onto an open ridge covered by high grass, and it was nice to get warmed up by the sunshine after the chill air of the forest. The spoor led us through a dry riverbed and up to another ridge, and here we came upon dung heap number two. The droppings were still smoking.

We took a short rest and examined our rifles. Winston took his own .450 Holland and Holland and I had Juma behind me with the .600 Jeffrey. He loathed that gun; it is accurate enough, he says, but kills whoever has to carry it. It weighs fifteen lbs. We took up the pursuit again. First went a tracker, then myself, with Winston close behind me. The rest were told to wait behind for ten minutes and then follow us. If they found a branch from a tree barring the path they were to stop there and only move forward to join us if they heard shots fired.

The spoor took us down a steep incline and at the bottom of this we could hear the babble from a stream. We descended slowly—no twigs must be broken, no stones must be dislodged and set in motion. After a while we could glimpse the silver ribbon of the stream and, where it widened out to a pool, we found our rhino voluptuously rolling over from one side to the other.

The tracker sidestepped and gave way. Juma handed me the fifteen pounds of steel, and Winston and I crept forward by ourselves. We still couldn't see the horn; perhaps, after all, this wasn't the one we had been looking for. The light was still fairly dim down there in the riverbed and we were not quite within shooting range. We advanced, step by step, gazing at the ground and at overhanging branches, now and then taking a quick look at our quarry. At last the horn came into view, standing up like a great bow from his nose—the best I had ever seen.

When we were a hundred yards from him, he rose from his mudbath and strolled leisurely up the path on the other side. If he continued in the same direction he would pass within fifty yards of where we stood. Quite right, here he came. A last reassuring whisper to Winston, "Take it easy," and then the report from the heavy rifle. The bullet hit, but did not kill, and he rushed up the slope. We ran up to the spoor and found some blood, and a little further on more from the lungs.

Soon the rest of the men arrived, and we decided to wait for an hour so as not to disturb him in case he had entered some thicket.

The lunch was good, but the appetite bad. The uncertainty was hanging like an ominous cloud over our heads, and not even a stiff "gin-and-french" managed to raise our spirits.

When the hour had passed, we took up the spoor again. It was easy to follow, as he had kept to the path, at first up to the ridge and then into the forest, but there he left the well-trodden trail. Evidently his speed had been reduced and we began to find more and more blood. One lair was pretty well soaked and further on he had swerved and gone down towards the stream in the valley. In one place, the spoor showed how he had staggered, in another how he had fallen down but got up again. At last we came to a wide sort of slide, edged on both sides by uprooted young trees and broken bush, and when we reached the precipice we could from there see, down by the stream, the great gray shape of the rhinoceros. He was dead, but was the horn undamaged by the violent dive he had taken?

Within a moment we were standing by our quarry. The giant had landed on his stomach and the head fallen between his forelegs. The horn, the longest I had ever seen (it measured thirty-two and a half inches), was pointing skywards. The natives were jubilant and I gave the beaming Winston a congratulatory slap on the back. We finished our lunch, now with better appetite, and went back to the camp.

The bush telegraph works quickly, and soon the entire village population had gathered at our camp. Presently the dancing commenced, the warriors performing round one bonfire, the women round another. Graceful movements in time to the rhythmic songs—brown supple bodies, swinging hips, and enticing voices. The flames threw fantastic moving shadows up towards the treetops. There was a festive atmosphere all around and dormant feelings came alive again.

The stirring beat of the drums accompanied the songs and added to the general gaiety, and in the native camp the fleshpots bubbled, sending up white and fragrant clouds of smoke that disappeared among the dark trees. Beer arrived in earthen pots and great calabashes—a wake was being held for "the big one," the old one, the one the *mtoto ya kingi** didn't get! Wahoga† and Bwana Americani were the heroes of the day.

And so at last two happy hunters fell asleep after a glorious day in a piece of country as beautiful and scenic as God has ever created.

There was no great urge to rise early when I called Winston the following morning. We had decided to move the camp some ten miles nearer to the Escarpment. There, along the Babati—Ndareda stretch, the gradient is very steep and there is an almost vertical fall of thirteen hundred feet. With great difficulties someone has managed to construct a motor road from Ndareda to Mbulu through narrow gorges and along precipitous mountainsides. Even if the road is not entirely suited to heavy traffic, I do think this five-mile-long ascent is one of the most scenic routes I have ever experienced. I had chosen the site for our next camping place just where the road reaches its highest elevation; from there you have a splendid view of the great cone of Mount Hanang keeping watch over the entire valley and being reflected in the waters of a small soda lake at the foot of the Rift wall. A small cloud nearly always hovers over the summit of this 11,000 foot volcano, possibly serving as a memento of bygone days when fire and lava were hurled westwards for many miles. Extensive ridges made up of lava rock and ashes give evidence of the fact that even in those days the wind nearly always blew from the east.

We took only one truck with us and sent it ahead with our simple camp equipment to the new site. Raymond had by then joined us, and the three of us decided to walk cross-country in the hope of finding new tracks. With the truck I sent two local scouts who knew all about the rhinoceros with the dragging foot. We took two gunbearers, two trackers, and two porters for our provisions.

We started at seven o'clock, and it was fresh and chilly that early in the morning. The sun, however, had already risen above the edge of the forest and its warming rays were gilding the hillsides and glades. I don't

---

Mtoto ya kingi—the king's son, i.e., the Prince of Wales.
†*Wahoga*, the Kikuyu name for Blix, was known to all Africans. Translated roughly as *wild goose*, Blix always maintained the name had been given him because of the fact he never stayed for very long at one place; less charitable friends thought it alluded to his slightly rolling gait.

know if you've ever walked the forest path between the mission and Ndareda. The vegetation is mostly wild olive and the pretty reddish-brown trunks grow like wind-driven oaks, with the same silvery leafage you find in the groves in Greece. From the branches and lianas of the giant trees in the rain forest gray-green lichen and moss hang down like enormous beards, and there the vervet monkey and colobus have their playground. Screeching green pigeons flutter in the foliage and doves of all kinds are plentiful.

Just before we entered the forest proper a flight of francolin shot up and we got three to give us a change in our diet. We had left Saleh behind at the mission to prepare yesterday's trophy. Winston wanted the forefeet, the horn, the head mask, and, in addition, the hide of the back to be cut up in two pieces for the making of two tabletops. When they are ground and polished they come out faintly transparent and look like amber.

On our way we found numerous buffalo, rhinoceros, and elephant spoor. Otherwise there is not a lot of game in this forest. Here and there we found footprints of dik-dik, bushbuck, and giant forest hog, and in open moist glades there were spoor of waterbuck and reed buck.

When we had been walking for a couple of hours we suddenly heard the trumpeting of an elephant. In this area there were no very big bulls, but there is always something interesting and exciting about elephants, so we turned off in the direction of the sound. Presently we could hear the snapping of twigs and the usual flapping of their ears. There was a small meadow between the animals and ourselves and we cautiously crept up to the edge. There we were met by a spectacle I'll never forget. The meadow was about ten acres in size and sloped down from the forest. In the center of this small field a spring was bubbling up. It was surrounded by a tiny swamp overgrown with star grass and tall copper-colored flowers tinged with yellow. In the bright sunshine one got the impression that the entire swamp was in flames. In the middle of this burning display of color two colossal buffalo bulls were standing gazing at the feeding elephants as if they were surprised to see them eating branches and not grass like themselves. Two younger animals were turning their backs towards us, and one small calf was keeping close to its mother as it received succulent broken-off young twigs from her.

Crouching down, we remained a long time watching this fascinating spectacle. Then suddenly the buffalo became restless and one of them started pawing the ground and throwing his head from side to side. I handed Raymond his good friend the .450 Holland and Holland and he pointed at the shoulder blade. The range was about eighty yards, and he fired. The bullet hit slightly high, but the animal fell like a stone. The other bull rushed diagonally towards us, alerted by the echo from the forest behind. "Point of shoulder!" Raymond cried, and the second shot followed; the bull collapsed like the first one.

The elephants pelted through the forest down into the valley. At first there was a roar as if a forest fire had swept through—and one could hear trees falling in their wake. Then everything became quiet. They were standing still, listening, but at last we could hear them, stealing away. It sounded as if a gentle breeze were passing through the reeds.

Away, away! Man, the disturber of the peace, is here!

The buffalo were magnificent. We sent word to the nearest village for men to come and collect the meat—we ourselves only wanted the horns and the undercuts. The horns would be taken care of by Saleh. The goddess of the hunt had again smiled on us, and in the best of spirits we continued on to the camp.

We arrived at noon. The truck had arrived, the tent was pitched, and a table and chairs had been put up in the shadow of a tree, and from there we had a fine view of the valley below us.

Far to the left I could spot our house on Cooper's farm, and the coffee plantation gleamed a bright green in the multicolored palette that was spread below and in front of us. The soda lake at our feet glimmered silvery white, with patches of pink here and there—flocks of flamingoes. The slopes of Mount Hanang were shot with green of all shades, from the dark of the rain forest to the light clear of the bamboo, and on the farthest rim of the volcano the newly germinated grass glittered like beeches in the spring. Around the villages there were fields of maturing maize and newly ploughed furrows of red humus. In the extensive pastures, where children were herding multicolored cattle and goats, grew large patches of blue and white convolvulus.

At the foot of Mount Hanang a few eland were grazing and below us in the stony thorn scrub a herd of impala—the most graceful of all African antelopes—could be seen skipping about.

At two o'clock our scouts came back, telling us they had found the spoor of the lame rhinoceros but also that it was an hour's walk from there and had been made overnight. Raymond, however, was keen on taking up the spoor, even if the chances of finding him were slight.

At this point some natives from the other side of the valley arrived with the news that they had found kudu—and roan antelopes and big herds of impala. Winston therefore took the truck and, with Juma as guide, went off to look for them while Raymond and I started to make preparations for the rhino hunt.

In this type of rugged terrain with dense aloe thickets and a network of wait-a-bit thorn scrub it soon became obvious that we could expect an exhausting afternoon. There was plenty of rhino spoor and we had to be on the alert at all times. In country like that it would be almost fatal to meet a rhino head-on, as he with his built-in armor plating and terrific strength could penetrate the thickest vegetation faster than we could pass through long grass. At last we came upon the spoor we were searching for; it was fresh from the morning and the imprint clearly showed the "drag" from one of his legs. In moist and loose soil he had had difficulties lifting this leg, and one could easily follow the groove it had made in the ground. Evidently he had during the night been down to the soda lake and was now on his way up to the highlands.

During our walk we had seen half a dozen different rhinos, but none of them with good horns. We decided to follow an easier route home and go back to the soda lake the next morning and look for fresh tracks there.

We were fairly tired by the time we got back to camp, where we found Winston already arrived. He had got a good impala and seen in the distance two kudu females and one bull, but as the wind had been unfavorable he had not been able to get within shooting range. Juma was very excited and explained that the bull had had a very good head—better than the one I had shot here some time ago (forty-eight inches). With a bit of luck they should be able to get him tomorrow, particularly as Juma knew of a path which, if the wind was right, would get them right up to the place where they had seen the animals and where there was both water and good grazing. Juma is a real hunter, always optimistic and eager to get away—rather like a retriever when he's seen the gun.

Just before I went to sleep I heard two lions roaring in the valley and, in the direction of where the buffalo had been killed, the hyenas were calling each other to begin the feast. From the village came the dull, rhythmical beat of the drums, and now and then the sound of women's voices could be heard rather like the whispering of a distant organ.

It was quite a bit warmer there at an altitude of approximately five thousand feet. The night was glorious and the stars twinkled like jewels on dark blue velvet.

By half past five the next morning we were drinking our tea, and an hour later we said good-bye to Winston, who left together with the ever-busy Juma, who was in great form anticipating a fruitful day. Winston had chosen a few local friends to come along, as they were familiar with that particular area; he promised me that they would not go after lion, leopard, buffalo, or rhino and that they would be back before dark. Judging by his expression he was obviously determined to return with a great surprise in the form of a truck full of meat and trophies.

Soon we ourselves started off for the soda lake. The sun had just risen above the crest of Mount Hanang and the soda on the lake glistened like newly driven snow. Flocks of flamingoes fluttered from shore to shore, and the wide belt of yellow thorn trees that framed the lake shone brightly with their tender foliage. In the treetops perched thousands of white egrets and a few kavirondo cranes danced in a ring by the shore. Their hoarse cries echoed far up the mountains.

We followed the western shore of the lake and presently spotted a rhino about a mile and half away standing in the dry soda crust. Beyond him, and still further out, we glimpsed another one. They seemed to be enjoying a bit of sun before going back to the shade and safety of the bush. The sunshine not only warms them but also hardens the mud clinging to their bodies after the morning's wallow, thus rendering the attacks from parasites less effective.

The soda has an acrid and sulphurous smell but makes our footsteps less audible, rather like walking on fresh snow. The rhino furthest away looked like he had a good horn, but the field glasses could as yet not determine whether it indeed was "the lame one." We made a detour through the yellow thorn trees, so as not to disturb the nearest animal, and from these came out on the lake again. The big bull had now started to walk towards the forest, and I advised Raymond to fire. The first bullet hit him a fraction too far behind the shoulder, but the second dropped him.

No "drag" was visible in his tracks, so it was not the one we had been looking for. Nevertheless it was a good trophy—the tape measure showed twenty-nine inches. Photos were taken, a runner was sent to camp, and everybody was pleased and satisfied. Raymond and I sat down on a fallen thorn tree to rest and sent out a few scouts to look for other tracks in the white soda. It was here I had heard lions the night before and it also looked the ideal territory for leopard. Terrain like that, with crevices and bush-covered cliffs alternating with tall thorn trees, is the ideal habitat for baboons—and the baboon ranks tops on the leopard's list of favorite foods.

Soon the men from camp arrived—Saleh was with them to deal with the dead rhino—and at the same time the trackers arrived. They had, however, not found anything of interest.

We then followed the southern edge of the lake. Here a couple of streams flowed into the saltpan. Numerous mallard and teal were swimming about in a freshwater pool and a flock of Egyptian geese were waddling up and down the shore. Duck is a welcome addition to the camp menu and a fat roasted teal is something even the most spoiled gourmet would appreciate. After about an hour's wade in the shallows we got a couple of geese and two brace of teal and Raymond shot a good impala and a bushbuck with an excellent head—an old buck—almost completely black.

By sundown we were back in camp again and could stretch our tired legs in front of a warming bonfire. We hadn't sat there for long before we could hear the approaching truck and a few minutes later it came around the corner of the road. A kudu head was tied to the front seat, and in the back the natives were performing a sort of war dance—the hunt must have been very successful. Juma was the first to jump off; the triumphant expression on his face defies description. He shook with eagerness to tell us how everything had happened—but we first wanted to hear Winston's undoubtedly more sober version. When he had got himself settled in a camp chair and washed down some of the dust with a whisky and soda he was ready to tell his story:

"From the road we followed a path which led us to some huts and further on to a point west of the ridge where we had seen the animals yesterday. From there we followed a valley with stony outcrops and thick scrub on both sides. The ground was covered with loose stones and we had to proceed with the utmost caution, Juma in the lead scanning each bush with field glasses. After an hour's walk he stopped, and from his broken English I gathered that he had seen a kudu but had only had a brief glimpse of his head. He was, however, convinced that this was the big one from yesterday, as the tips of the horns reached well above the tops of the surrounding bushes—all this was accompanied by vivid gesticulations. We should now wait there till three o'clock—Juma pointed at the sun—and then we should climb a steep cliff behind us from where we would be able to see the top of the next ridge. The kudu would lie down and go to sleep—gestures—and between three and four o'clock he would start grazing again—more gestures. The plan sounded feasible, but the range from the cliff to where the kudu was now standing was long—over two hundred yards. Juma, however, thought this would do.

"I had no better suggestion to offer, and we went back to the truck. Juma said a few words to the driver and we started off. I didn't know where we were going, but it was obvious Juma had something in mind. We crossed the entire valley and entered an open forest of African oak with an undergrowth of broad-leafed grass. Here we came upon a bigger road, which from the map I understood to be the main Arusha–Dodoma highway. Going north, we followed this for a while and presently we spotted a herd of roan antelopes. They stood still for a moment watching the car, but then went off. They all had horns, but Juma categorically declared: No males.

"We continued down into a depression, and here we left the car and climbed up a hill. From there we had a good view of the ravines leading down to the valley. Suddenly Juma was transformed into something that looked like a leaping panther. He crawled up to me and pointed at a precipice some eight hundred yards away. I raised the field glasses and there indeed stood an almost coal-black roan bull, peacefully feeding on the tender new grass. The wind was against us, so we had to creep back in the cover of high ground in order to get closer to the place where he was standing. Juma was angelic in his patience and in the care he took to get me there silently. He removed twigs and other obstacles in our way, and so we went on step by step. We reached the ridge and carefully took a look over the top. There, opposite us, stood the roan bull, still grazing peacefully. Slowly I raised the rifle, using a small thorn tree as support. I hit him in the center of the shoulder, he made a rush forward for some seventy yards, and then he fell down dead.

"Juma was overjoyed and took snuff, so one could see brown rivulets running down from the corners of his mouth. 'Wahoga very pleased,' he said, and he disappeared at great speed in the direction of the parked vehicle after having indicated his wish for me to go up to the fallen quarry. Imagine the surprise I felt when a bit later I saw the truck coming up weaving between trees and boulders. It did take some time, but it got there in the end. Having quartered the animal we managed to get it aboard.

"The sun had passed its zenith long ago and we went back to wait for the kudu. The whole thing went off exactly as Juma had told us it would. It was well past four o'clock when the great horns appeared above the bushes. The kudu bull grabbed a blade of grass here and there as he walked slowly in our direction. After a few minutes, the entire animal came within our view. What a wonderful sight: the dark slate-gray skin so perfectly camouflaged by the cross stripes; the noble line of his head; the big calm eyes; the permanently twitching ears; the beautifully chiseled spiral horns with their glistening ivory tips.

"I fired at a range of one hundred and fifty yards; I don't have to say any more—as he is now dead. Juma insisted on removing the neck, skin, and head, and I now understand that even then he had planned this triumphant return to the camp."

This surely has been Juma's day, and I can only compare his pleasure to that shown by my old pointer "Brans" at home after I had shot several brace of quail for him. The next day we returned to the main camp, where we were received with great rejoicing. Champagne with the dinner, cigars with the coffee, accounts of past events and stories until early morning. If only you had been there.

All my love,
Blix

In camp, April

My darling Cockie,

I am now camped closed to the big game reserve which is bounded by Lake Albert to the west, the Victoria Nile to the north, and a line running from Murchison Falls to Masindi to the east. The local natives have been greatly plagued by marauding elephants. In the spring big herds wander over the cultivated fields, trampling down the newly germinated maize and uprooting banana groves. The government has issued a license for me to shoot here in order to teach the elephant a lesson and make him return to the great expanse of land which for many years has been his habitat, where he can walk about undisturbed by anyone and nature has provided him with every requirement. Therefore there should be no need for him to take his food from the natives.

This part of the country has always fascinated me. One cannot help but think back to the days when Speke and Baker, in spite of hostile natives, alone succeeded in penetrating the area in search of the sources of the Nile. In Masindi one can still view the tree under which Baker put up his tent. It was along these paths that he and his wife, opposed by thousands of spear-carrying natives, had to shoot themselves free in order to get back to their main camp. At this time Livingstone was staying at Kasenyi, on the southwestern shore of Lake Albert. From the high country south of Masindi, Baker saw this wonderful lake framed by the distant blue mountains for the first time—completely unaware of the fact that the old missionary, missing for so long, was camped only a couple of days' march away. (If you haven't already read Samuel Baker's book *The Source of the Nile* you should do so.)

The whole of this area is also historically renowned from the days when the king of Uganda, Kabarega, fought his bloody battles against the dreaded ruler of the tribes from the fertile lands on the other side of the lake and river. At the time when Baker was here the population was numerous; then, however, the sleeping sickness struck and some districts had to be completely evacuated in order to limit the spread of this ravaging disease. Even today science has unfortunately not been able to solve this great African problem, although progress has been made in the curing of the sickness.

It is beautiful here in April. Everything is green; the verdure of the growing grass and the new foliage of the trees is overwhelming. It rains every afternoon and the chocolate-brown soil gives out a smell of moist humus and fertility. Topographically the terrain consists of high ground of great sweeping ridges furrowed by valley and ravines where rivers and streams flow between trees, swinging palms, and groves of wild bananas. Woodlands of a few hundred acres alternate with smaller plains where solitary giant trees break the monotony. These are remnants from the time when the country was completely covered with forest, long before humans started their pioneering and—after the population had retreated—the grass had taken over where formerly fertile fields had produced bananas, maize, and ground nuts. These plains burn every year and each grass fire pushes the forest boundary back, leaving behind the odd hardy tree and scattered clumps of bushes with a peculiar corklike bark that is resistant to the most extreme heat. Now these are in full blossom and the brick-red flowers give color to the plains—rather like poppies in a corn field.

Heavy black clouds are mounting up on the horizon and here and there the rain is pouring down—grayish-white mists beneath the dark mass. Long rolling thunder is now almost continuous. In this iron-rich country one can see the flashes of lightning coming down in thick slashes, seeking contact with the ground. Yesterday, when I was on my way back from a short reconnaissance, I was almost blinded by a tremendous flash which struck a solitary giant of a tree standing less than a hundred yards away. The entire top of the tree was split and two colossal branches were torn off and thrown a long way from the trunk. The sight was photographed in my mind and I shall never forget this impressive experience.

I have only got two boys with me, Abedi and Juma Nandi, and my entire equipment consists of a light camp bed, two blankets, a sleeping bag, and a small one-man tent. I've packed the tent in my rucksack, so I only need four porters to move my luggage. The packs only weigh thirty lbs. each, so we can take everything with us. In the way of provisions, I have only taken sugar, rice, flour, and tea. Potatoes, eggs, chickens, and bananas I get from the natives every day in exchange for all the meat I provide them with.

According to the reports from the natives there should be plenty of elephant about; they talk about big herds of more than a hundred animals and here and there occasional bulls. I don't think I'll stay in this area for more than a month, as the grass becomes too long, but later I intend to move on, into the Congo, on the other side of Lake Albert. At present the price of ivory is fairly good and, in accordance with my license, I retain half and the government half. Michael Moses, my old friend in Kampala, looks after the sales and hands out necessary advances. He believes the marketing price for next month's sales will be sixteen and a half shillings per lb. for Masindi.

All my love
Blix

CHAPTER
5

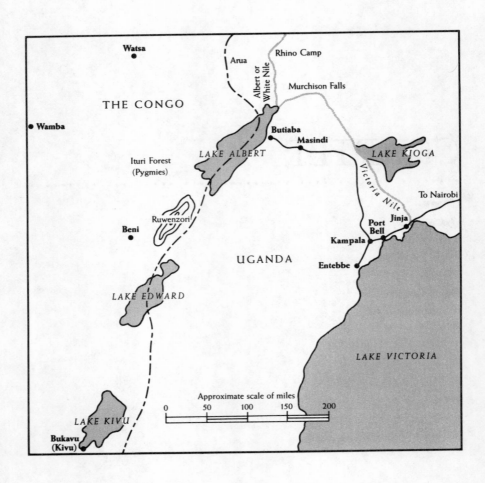

Watsa

THE CONGO

Wamba

Arua

Rhino Camp

Albert or
White Nile

Murchison Falls

Butiaba

LAKE ALBERT

Masindi

LAKE KIOGA

Ituri Forest
(Pygmies)

Victoria Nile

To Nairobi

Ruwenzori

Jinja

Beni

Port
Bell

Kampala

UGANDA

Entebbe

LAKE EDWARD

LAKE VICTORIA

Approximate scale of miles

0   50   100   150   200

LAKE KIVU

Bukavu
(Kivu)

· ·

Masindi, Friday

My darling Cockie,

Today, I shot my first two elephants. We had spent the night close to
some remote huts, where the elephants already had caused extensive
damage. The three-foot-tall maize had in several places been eaten and
trampled down and in the groves the bananas had been thrown to the
ground and the fronds chewed up. The wild fig trees—here cultivated
because of the use made of the bark—were broken and uprooted. There
was great joy when I arrived and neighbors appeared from all directions,
all with the same complaints against the silent gray monsters.

In the evening the drums were brought and dancing commenced, con-
tinuing far into the night, until it came to a stop with the arrival of the
elephants. The first thing we heard was the sharp crack of a banana tree
being broken, then another one, followed by the characteristic tummy
rumblings and loud munching and chewing noises. Trumpet calls from
farther down the valley indicated the approach of more elephants. The
drums were put away, more wood added to the fires, and torches were lit.
Carrying these, a couple of men sneaked down to the banana groves.
Having arrived, they started swinging their torches overhead till sparks
were flying in all directions, at the same time screaming and shouting in
an effort to drive the animals away. The marauders took absolutely no
notice and continued their destructive work regardless. More men with
torches joined the first ones and the noise became louder. Possibly all this
had some effect in checking the advance of the approaching herd, but
none at all on those already in the vicinity, and throughout the night we
could hear their chewing and the repeated thuds as more trees and saplings were torn down. In the distance, lots of torches glowed in the night
and shouts and yells from neighboring villages indicated that they had

been attacked as well—obviously there was no shortage of elephants in the area.

Naturally I preferred to get big tusks, but as the object of the exercise was to teach the elephants a lesson, one couldn't be too choosy.

A new day was upon us: a cool dawn with mists hanging over the valley and dew on the grass. Silvery veils, glimmering under the first rays of sunshine, skimmed along the edge of the forest, the sky was clear, and the air clean and fragrant after yesterday's rain. Whilst Abedi made tea and packed the equipment, Juma, the men from the village, and myself went to see what really had happened during the night. Judging by the tracks, there had been seven elephants in the raiding party—two cows, two calves, two bulls, and one half-grown animal. The imprints were sharp and defined in the soft soil, and one could clearly see where they had left the cultivated areas and crossed the valley towards a copse on the next ridge.

It was a radiantly beautiful morning, and the bird life was intense. There was chirping and twittering everywhere. Hundreds of weaver birds were extremely busy building in a big tree standing between the huts. Their nests are ingenious masterpieces, hanging down in clusters from the weakest points of outer branches. The funnel-formed entrances face downwards, preventing cat, weasel, or even the most supple snake from getting at their eggs or young ones. Jet-black widow birds with glistening plumage fluttered in wild love dances over the grasslands further out. Screeching flocks of green pigeon moved from one clump of trees to the next, and high up in the tops of giant trees one could glimpse black-and-white colobus monkeys searching for buds and young shoots, swinging from branch to branch in elegant arcs and calling each other with their peculiar creaking guttural voices.

The sun, enormous and apricot-colored, had now risen above the horizon, and we followed the elephant tracks into the forest. Here the ground had been trodden hard by the big animals and the trees dyed red by mud from their bodies. Old and fresh heaps of dung could be seen everywhere; it was very evident that this was a favorite haunt of the elephant. It was difficult to track in the half light, so we decided to make a detour around the edge of the forest to see if possibly more animals had entered.

As we were rounding a corner of the woods we came upon twelve animals standing out in the open, basking in the morning sun. None of them had acceptable tusks, so, with a favorable wind, we managed to pass between them and the forest, which here stretched up towards the top of the ridge. We carefully avoided a small herd of buffalo, then leaving their night pastures for the dim and cool rain forest.

From a tall antheap on top of the ridge we could look down into the next valley. By a stream edged by dark trees stood a solitary bull elephant, flapping his ears to keep the flies away. His tusks gleamed white in the sharp morning light and I estimated their weight at sixty-five lbs. each. To get any nearer, however, would have been tricky, as the wind was blowing from us, and we had to make a long detour down into the valley and then up again on the other side, following the windings of the stream. I had brought a 6.5mm Mannlicher and a .450 Holland and Holland (as well as a .22 Winchester for birdshooting). The bull was still there when we got to the place we had aimed for. I told the villagers in my retinue to stay behind, and with Juma, who was carrying the heavy rifle, I started creeping forward. If I could get near enough it was my intention to go for the brain with the Mannlicher so as not to disturb other animals with the louder report from the heavy rifle.

I had managed to get within thirty yards of him when he suddenly raised his trunk. His enormous ears were stretched tautly like sails, and he stood broadside-on, listening intently. The small bullet hit just the front of the earhole and he dropped on the spot. The hind legs collapsed first, then he went down on his knees—dead.

Immediately after the shot, there was a sudden commotion in the bushes down by the stream. Yet another big bull emerged and started to stroll down the valley. The range was about ninety yards. I exchanged the Mannlicher for the heavier rifle and rapidly fired two shots. Just as I was reloading he staggered, took a few more tottering steps, and fell on his side with a great thud.

Both bulls carried thick, heavy tusks, so from the ivory point of view the morning had been satisfactory. The villagers with me hurried back to spread the glad news and to call up men for the chopping out of the tusks and to take care of the meat. We continued along the valley, and through the field glasses I could spot more elephants higher up. Hartebeest and waterbuck were numerous everywhere and along the water courses we saw smaller herds of Uganda cob. I intended to shoot a buck for Juma and Abedi as soon as we got closer to the next village, where I planned to camp for the night. There were plenty of francolin and guinea fowl about and I shot a francolin with the .22. I had provided meat for the people in the area and now I wanted to make a thorough survey of the elephant herds in the vicinity before I shot the next one.

By two o'clock it had started to cloud over and the sound of thunder in the distance made us take the shortest route back to the village. Soon we discovered a few columns of smoke further to the south and a narrow path led us to a cultivated area surrounded by half a dozen huts. Only a few old people were at home; the rest had gone to collect the meat from the dead elephants but were expected back before dark.

I arranged for wood and water to be collected and the tent was put up. One of the smaller huts had been evacuated and would serve as kitchen and sleeping quarters for Juma and Abedi. At dusk I went out with the .22, and got quite close to the banana grove. I shot a red duiker for the pot.

The villagers returned just after dark, loaded with meat. Several bonfires were lit and some of the men placed the drums in an open place between the huts. There were eight of these in varying sizes, made out of hollow tree trunks and covered by tautly stretched skins. The first beats were sounded, and some half-grown children began hesitantly to dance. A few young men joined in and soon the circle of dancers widened. Measured mark-time march intermingled with rhythmic leaps, either straight up and down or towards either side; monotonous but strangely stirring. In this way it was to continue all night.

Soon the place was crowded with people. Young girls with Venus-like bodies, mothers whose full breasts smackingly kept time to the music—a waving mass of swinging hips and rolling stomachs. All joined in and as time passed their enthusiasm rose. The songs became more and more lively and the tread harder. In the fluttering light from the flames the warm bodies glistened like polished copper and clouds of dust wrapped the ecstatic crowd like a snug veil.

I sat and watched these happy children of nature for a long time but finally tiredness overtook me and I rolled into my blanket and fell asleep.

At dawn the following morning Abedi came with tea and fresh scones. We parked our belongings, and by the time the sun rose over the horizon we were on the march again.

We were accompanied by a couple of young villagers who claimed to know of other herds of elephants and said there were some good bulls with them. The sky was overcast and dense cumulus clouds were mounting in white masses against the leaden ceiling. The atmosphere was close and stifling.

We followed a well-trodden path, winding between plots of growing maize, millet, simsim, sweet potatoes, pumpkins, and well-tended cotton fields. The low cotton bushes are about two feet tall and their foliage is rather like currants; the flowers look a bit like polyantha roses. Now and then one glimpsed a hut inside the banana groves and some of the fields were framed by orderly rows of wild fig. These trees are debarked and the bark is then hammered out by small clubs made of ivory until the thick skin becomes soft and pliable and can be used as cloth. The material is then colored red, white, and blue with different vegetable dyes and the resulting product is hard-wearing and durable—as long as it doesn't rain. The men use it as a kind of trousers by drawing a piece up between their legs and fastening it around their hips with a belt; the overhang is then draped in broad pleats. Judging by the straddle-legged gait of the men, however, the garment can't be all that comfortable to wear.

Flowers gave light to the young grass. African violets of many shades, delphinium and lobelia and splendid gladioli, varying in color from yellow to brick-red. The country was teeming with guinea-fowl and I saw flocks of as many as fifty birds.

At about nine o'clock we came upon fresh elephant spoor and these we followed up a wooded ridge. Further on these were joined by others and the tracks led us through thinly wooded terrain out into open bush country.

Old grass from last year, beaten down by rain and wind, was growing in large patches and providing shelter for the new crop, now germinating. Here the elephant have had their haunts for a long time and they had made well-trodden paths in all directions. Pretty palms were growing in scattered clumps, the trunks straight as arrows with spreading tops from which clusters of ripening fruit were hanging. These are as big as cabbages, orange in color, and have a pleasant smell of apple. The natives eat them after having beaten their fleshy part to a pulp with a piece of wood. Personally I think they are a bit too stringy and the taste is fairly bitter. The elephants, however, love them and there are well-trodden paths from one palm to the next. Here they wander on their morning stroll, picking up what has fallen down during the night.

At eleven o'clock we spotted the first elephants, a herd of about a hundred animals resting in the shade of some big trees. We climbed a small hill some five hundred yards away and were able to watch them through the field glasses. I couldn't discover more than three or four small bulls; the rest were cows and calves. However, with such a great number about there must be the odd big bull, so we continued without disturbing the herd.

From the hill we had noticed a small copse less than a mile further on, and we headed in that direction. The rain had as yet not caught us, but it was pouring all along the horizon.

Just as we were rounding the end of a thicket next to the copse where the elephants were standing, we came upon a sight that I'll remember for a long time. Less than two hundred yards from the edge of the woods eleven big bulls were standing in the grass half asleep and leisurely flapping their big ears. One or two of them were sucking up red dust with their trunks and then spraying their backs and necks in order to keep the irritating and persistent insects away. The white cattle egrets on their backs looked even brighter against the background of blue-black rain-clouds. Four of the bulls carried very long and pretty tusks, one short and thick, and the remaining six only average; however, it was all good ivory.

It was difficult to decide on the best plan of campaign. How would they react after the first shot was fired? Rush out in the open bush country or disappear into the forest for cover? At first, I considered the possibility of letting the natives go around them and then drive them past me, but that would run the risk of having them pass out of range, or packing together so tightly that it would be difficult to pick one's target. I therefore decided to walk straight at them where they stood, and took only Juma with me. I sent the guides and porters back to some high trees which they could climb in case of emergency. I then managed, without incident, to get within a hundred yards of the nearest. Unfortunately, this was not the biggest—that one was another twenty yards away. The egrets had now spotted us and were flying uneasily to and fro, and the elephants understood that something was wrong. Their enormous ears were stretched to the limit and their raised trunks were probing and testing the wind. We were lying motionless, crouching in the grass, and by and by the birds quieted down—it would have been better if they had left altogether.

About thirty yards from the nearest one there was an antheap, and we had to get there for cover. Step by step we crept forward, all the time watching any movement by the quarry and being careful not to give our position away by snapping twigs or rustling the dry grass. Nobody who has not been in a similar situation can imagine the excitement one feels when getting so close to those giants. Should we be discovered, there would be no protection, not a tree, to hide behind.

We reached the antheap and found the top too narrow to stand on, but from the broad base I got a clear view of the elephants. The biggest now stood about fifty yards away, the two biggest after him a bit to the right,

Hans and Bror, 1887, Nasbyholm.
(*Baron Hans von Blixen-Finecke*)

Hans and Bror, 1890, Nasbyholm.
(*Baron Hans von Blixen-Finecke*)

Early travel poster advertising the
delights of East Africa.

The Blixen farm in Nairobi in 1915.
(*G.F.V. Kleen*)

Bror and Karen Blixen with two
lionesses shot on their first safari in
1914. (*G.F.V. Kleen*)

Karen Blixen with her two favorite
deerhounds, Dusk and Dawn.
(G.F.V. Kleen)

Bror Blixen's first elephant. *(Ulf Aschan)*

The Norfolk Hotel, Nairobi,
c. 1918. It was known as "The
House of Lords." (*Jacqueline Hoogterp*)

and the smaller ones to the left, nearer the woods. The big one stood with his hindquarters pointed diagonally towards me, and I decided to wait until he turned broadside-on, when I could chance a brain shot with the Mannlicher. If the others should rush towards the woods after I had fired, the two on the right would have to pass me within range. Minutes went by, my heart was pounding, and Juma's eye looked like a tiger's ready to pounce.

Then came the sound of thunder over the valley. The animals woke up and started to move about in a restless manner. The big one turned broadside-on. *Bang!* He sank to the ground, forelegs first—a bad sign. The others stood stock-still, testing the wind and at a loss what to do. The one farthest to the right received a bullet in the shoulder from the double-barreled rifle, and the next moment all of them were coming straight at us. From ten paces, I fired again at the one wounded last and he got the bullet in the forehead, checked, turned, and got the other barrel in the shoulder. He staggered, and I could see that he had had enough.

But what about the big one—he might get up again, so I rushed up to him. He threw his head about, tried to find support for his forelegs, fell with a great thud on his side, made another effort, and got to his knees. Another bullet and it was all over. Number two had stopped a couple of hundred yards further on. We silently followed him and saw him stagger, then, throwing up his trunk, he fell on his side with a last trumpet call.

While all this was going on there had been a lot of commotion in the forest, and we made signs to the approaching porters to stay with the dead elephants; we ourselves ran in among the trees. It was dark in there and, in the thick undergrowth, we couldn't see much. Cautiously we followed an elephant path and I just had time to get a glimpse of a couple of cows a bit ahead. We followed them thinking there surely would be more animals in that direction. Having arrived at the edge of the woods, we could see the whole herd moving off, already half a mile away.

We went back to the dead animals and inspected the tusks. I estimated that the bigger ones weighed just over a hundred lbs. and the smaller ones about sixty-five lbs. Then we cut off the tips of their tails. The natives make bracelets and other ornaments from the coarse and sparsely growing bristles.

Our guides told us that there were a few native huts one-and-a-half hour's walk from there and we decided to take the shortest route that would get us there. It had not started to rain yet, but it looked threatening.

As we were wading over a small stream at the bottom of a depression, a lone bull elephant came down the opposite slope at a brisk walk straight at us. He carried magnificent tusks, long and thick, and they gleamed snowy-white against his black body. Most elephants here are a reddish-brown, getting that color from the soil they spray themselves with, but this one must have taken a recent bath or been through a rain shower, as he was black and clean.

The wind blew from him towards us and if he continued in the same direction he would pass within thirty yards of us. Circumstances made it all too easy for the hunter. Both bullets from the heavy rifle hit him in the shoulder, and he went on for a short distance before he fell with a crash. The tusks were very good, however, and I estimated that they would weigh out at over a hundred lbs. each.

Then the rain started, not the sort of rain we are used to at home, but as if one had turned on the bathroom shower full blast. Within a few minutes the ground became saturated with water and very slippery, and in spite of the successful hunt, the men walked on in depressed silence under their light packs. It is a curious fact that though he must know the beneficial effect the rain has on his crops, most natives loathe to be out in a downpour. The path we were following soon became a torrent of foaming water and it became difficult to keep one's balance. Instead of the promised hour and a half, we had been on our way for nearly three when at last we came to some cultivated fields. From a small hill we could see banana groves and also some smoke spiraling up, so we knew it was someone's habitation. A bit later we heard a cock crowing and some goats braying and we arrived just as it was getting dark.

The inhabitants gathered round us; the guides explained who we were and told about the elephants, news that brought great rejoicing, and we were quickly offered the biggest hut.

The rain had eased off, and a faint sliver of light in the west gave hope of better weather for the evening. Presently a homey fire crackled on the floor of the hut, Juma got going with his maintenance of the guns, Abedi became busy with his pots and pans, and I got out a change of dry clothing and shoes.

The drums were sounded and the bush telegraph got functioning, spreading the news from village to village.

As soon as the water was boiling in the pot, I brewed myself some tea. Outside the door one of the guinea-fowl I had shot was being plucked, in a corner potatoes were being peeled, and on the fire the rice was bubbling. Some women brought bananas, eggs, and ground nuts. Abedi brought a bottle of simsim oil, which is excellent for cooking.

Later in the evening the rain stopped and the drums were brought out for dancing. A big bonfire was built in the middle of the village and I had a chair and small table placed in front of it. More and more people arrived and soon the dancing commenced. The elders were sitting in council over the distribution of the meat. I let the headman know that I wished my guides to get ample compensation for their work, and gave instructions for the tusks to be chopped out and brought to the hotel in Masindi.

I then talked to several natives from neighboring villages, questioning them about the elephants. All had stories to tell and each one tried to persuade me to visit his own village. There was a lot of muddled information and it was difficult to sort out what was truth and what was idle speculation.

I thought it best to take it easy for a few days and wait till I had more reliable news. After today's hunt, and bearing in mind all the hullabaloo that would occur by the dead elephants tomorrow, it was obvious that no more animals would be seen for some time within a radius of at least fifteen miles.

It would take some little time before I renewed my contact with elephants. In the meantime, I went down to Murchison Falls, one of the most grandiose sights I have ever visited. Perhaps not the falls themselves, but the area generally and the wildlife particularly. The Victoria Nile is here forced through a narrow mountain gorge and then surges in a wild roaring cascade down a five-hundred-yard-long incline and finally over a ninety-degree precipice. Below this there is a pool, and after the river has been forced through yet another gorge, it emerges into a larger and calmer pool. East of this there is a swamp separated from the pool by a sandspit built up by water at flood level.

The quantity of fish in the Nile is supposed to be greater than in any other river, and here, as in any other watercourse, the fish seek to go upstream in the spawning season. Murchison Falls, however, constitutes an obstacle which they cannot negotiate, and so they remain below in great masses, fin to fin.

This fantastic scenery should be painted, or put to music—not described on paper. The river rushes, with a roar like an express train entering a tunnel, through the mountain gorge, throwing up tremendous rapids that are forever being chased by those behind. The rays of sun break like flashes of lightning over the surface of the water, and above this blinding panorama there is a shimmer, in all the colors of the rainbow, hanging like a soft veil of foam over the cataract.

Cormorants hover above the waves in airy display, diving into the pool below with outstretched necks, appearing again, and then back to where the rapids are at their most violent. They soar side by side, they turn, they dive, they dance. The games of the wild, the ballet of the jungle, in one of the game sanctuaries of the world, where there are no reports of firearms and no traps set. In the pool below the booming cascade, the fish attempt to jump the rapids, in vain but repeatedly—like black streaks, they shoot up through the white masses of foam only to fall back again into the boiling steel-gray depths. A dance palace of the wilderness, where the orchestra plays without intermission and the spotlight on the colorful wings always changes in harmony with the shifting rays of sun and the flickering play of the shadows in the valley.

On the sandspit by the swamp lie crocodile next to crocodile, satiated, gorged, and immobile. They symbolize everything that is treacherous, repulsive, horrid, and malevolent—one of the many representatives from hell on this earth.

In the still waters below the rapids, hippopotamuses show their shapeless heads, others stand on rocky islets and on stones, their wet bodies gleaming in the sun. It is only between eight and nine o'clock in the morning and the heat has as yet not driven them to their favorite resting places, the calm depressions in the river bottom, where the current passes over them. Every five minutes they have to rise to the surface for air; only their nostrils become visible, and only for a few seconds, then they disappear again—the whole process as regular as our own breathing and just as instinctively automatic. Of all the animal constructions emanating from our Lord's drawing board this is possibly the most ingenious; a vegetarian mammal that in a hot climate grazes on land during the cool hours of the night, and then in the heat of the day lives in cool waters. Apart from the human being with his weapons, snares, and pitfalls, the hippo has no enemies. Even the crocodile doesn't dare touch the hippo's young, as just one chomp from his well-equipped jaws would finish off even the biggest of these monsters.

I very much wanted to get to the other side of the river, and my guides have promised that tomorrow they will fetch a canoe which they have hidden away a couple of hours' march downstream.

The vegetation here is partly woods, with wide strips of grass separating the different stands. Here also the old grass from last year has been burnt and the new green crop is already a foot tall. There are enormous elephant spoor and well-trodden buffalo paths cross each other everywhere.

As anticipated by my guides, herds of elephant and buffalo come down to the river for an afternoon dip. There the animals are quite undisturbed. The ravages of sleeping sickness have made it necessary for the government to evacuate the native population to other districts and nobody is allowed to hunt here. Even I am here without permission and at my own risk. Only jungle law is in force.

After I had woken up from my afternoon siesta, I watched two fish eagles, the most striking birds in the world, soar in wide circles over the river. A few hornbills flew with heavy, flapping wings over the treetops, baboons quarrelled, parrots chattered. After the sun passed its zenith and it became less hot, the jungle woke up. Then, suddenly, through the din from the rapids, a shrill trumpet blast was heard. The elephants were on their way! *"Iko! Iko!* [Here! Here!]," the man whispered, and pointed at the fringe of forest on the other side, and from out of the woods emerged in a long line these remnants from prehistoric times. In the lead was a cow with a very small calf, not much bigger than a dog, following her closely. They proceeded at a brisk walk and then stopped a short distance from the bank. They sniffed, turning from side to side, testing the wind with their supple trunks. Then the cow in front entered the water. She filled her trunk and sprayed her back and ears, then sniffed again—everything appeared to be quiet. The others couldn't wait any longer and with exaggerated strides moved ahead and walked into the shallow water. They drank and showered themselves, trumpeting with pleasure. Some of them played with their young, others rolled over on their sides and backs, beating the water into a frothy foam with their enormous ears. They enjoyed themselves and played in the shallows for a long time before going ashore again, where they stopped for a while, letting the water run off their bodies. Then, with long strides, they disappeared like ghosts to the pastures whence they came.

In the twilight a herd of buffalo, arrived. Uncertain, they stood on the shore for a while, sniffing and looking around. Then they trotted down to the water, slaked their thirst, and returned the same way, back to their own paradise.

A moment later, a gold-flecked streak slid through the reeds, a leopard. Cautiously he crept down to the shallowest spot and drank, lying on his stomach as he lapped up the water, all the time on the alert, since the crocodile in this element is his superior. Then he slowly went back and huddled up on a flat slab of stone which was still warm from the sun, licked himself clean and dry, and enjoyed a bit of siesta before the night hunt commenced.

In my small camp several fires gleamed in a friendly fashion, and the smoke rose peacefully against a darkening evening sky. Pots were bubbling in Abedi's kitchen and a delicious smell reached my nostrils. My chair had been placed by an improvised table made from empty cases and in front of me a small fire blazed invitingly. The roar from the river seemed to be even louder now, the crickets were tuning up and the bullfrogs were drumming away, and in the distance a lion was roaring.

For dinner I was given grilled Nile perch, the best of all freshwater fish, fried potatoes, an omelette made from ostrich eggs which the boys had found earlier in the day, and strong Uganda coffee. What more could anybody wish for, and what could be more fitting to the feelings of the moment?

About the Nile perch. Apart from being the most sporting freshwater fish in African waters, it is a great delicacy. He can weigh up to over two hundred lbs. but generally you get him at an average of forty-five lbs. You find him in all the rivers in the Congo basin and in the waters of the Nile system, but because of Murchison Falls, he has been unable to reach Lake Victoria or any waters east of there, with the exception of Lake Rudolph, to the northeast. In Lake Albert I have caught him several times and believe he is more numerous there than in any other location. For some extraordinary reason this fish seems to incur a tremendous rate of mortality at about the middle of the month of December. At that time of year, I have three times been to Lake Albert and on each occasion I have found thousands, maybe tens of thousands, of dead Nile perch, mostly in the range of twenty to forty-five lbs. Possibly this curious fact has something to do with the spawning season. Should the reason be a periodically recurring poisoning of the water (there is oil under the lake), other species of fish would also die; this, however, is not the case. Should an opportunity arise, I would very much like to visit other lakes where this fish lives to find out if this phenomenon occurs there at the same time. Interesting objects for such a survey would be the lakes Rudolph and Chad. The biggest Nile perch I've seen was on the Chari River by Fort Lamy near

Lake Chad; it was a fish speared by natives and weighed two hundred and twenty-five lbs.

As promised, the men turned up with the canoe at eight o'clock. It was a long hollowed-out tree trunk made from Uganda teak. This kind of craft is poled along the riverbank, paddles only being used in deeper water. The hippo constitutes quite a threat to the crew and the canoe, from which he has been hunted with harpoons for hundreds, maybe thousands, of years. They nearly always attack a canoe, sometimes employing their wide open jaws against the side of the craft and sometimes diving under it and upending it with their powerful backs, causing those aboard to be thrown into the water and the heavy boat to sink to the bottom. Once in the water, the natives became easy prey for the furious beasts seeking revenge for past misdeeds.

So now it was eight o'clock. I sat on the bank with field glasses and camera. Hundred of crocodiles were floating motionless, like moulded logs. They had finished their morning meal and were waiting for the heat of the day before crawling up on land to bask in the sun. Nothing disturbs them and the roar from the rapids and the constant buzzing of bird wings provide them with daily music.

I discussed with the crew of the canoe how best to get over to the other side without taking too much of a risk. The river was teeming with hippos and there was also a strong undertow. Should the boat for some reason capsize, we wouldn't have many seconds to live. We decided to cross at the upper end of the pool. Here there was a small backwater behind heaps of stone and just then no hippos could be seen near there. So, we set off, Juma and I and four paddlers. All was well, but near the bank we got into a shoal of crocodiles. Twice the paddles hit their backs and, with a lot of splashing, the monsters dived. We were all pleased when the canoe scraped bottom on the other side, where we tied up and then crept down to the swamp behind the cover of bushes and big boulders.

The panorama in front of us was almost unbelievable. The whole swamp was a mass of crawling crocodiles. Some of them had already climbed the sandspit and those that had dried off looked like dead gray tree trunks. They were lying with their jaws wide open, the underside of their throats showing pale yellow. Small black-and-white spotted warblers about the size of our starling were busily running up and down, inspecting the dentistry of the beasts and stopping whenever a remaining morsel of fish was found. This service was evidently appreciated by the gorged and half-asleep reptiles.

Within an imagined square I counted about one hundred crocodiles. The surface of this square was relatively small compared to the entire area, and I estimated that there must have been from two to three thousand animals in the swamp. We sat for a long time watching these unbelievably ugly, repellent, and dangerous beasts. What an enormous amount of fish must be consumed every day for the feeding of this crawling multitude. But maybe the day will come when it will be possible to put to good use the enormous quantity of fish available here and at the same time exterminate the totally useless crocodile.

Close to the bank a flock of spoon-billed storks were fishing, moving their heads in even sweeps from right to left just like men cutting grass with a scythe. Presumably they catch insects and small fish, which they filter through their spatulate bills. A big flock of whistling teal was squatting on a sandbank and about a dozen Egyptian geese were perched on some stones not far away. On the sunny side of the swamp three hippos were asleep in the shallow water, resting their heads on each other's backs. Everything was calm and quiet and the roar from the falls was monotonous and sleep-inducing.

I told the four men to sneak over to the other side of the swamp and there to make as much noise as possible. Screened by the vegetation, Juma and I crawled to a large slab of rock on a sandbank. After a while shouts and screams were heard and there was instant commotion in the swamp. In wild panic the crocodiles hurled themselves, big and small, towards the river. There wasn't room for them all and the bigger ones rushed over the smaller and weaker. There ensued a swarming and crawling of gray-green backs, yellow bellies dragging tails and bending legs; small, slanting eyes gleamed maliciously and in the half-open jaws flashed rows of the dreaded teeth. This nightmare lasted for ten minutes—then the swamp was completely empty. Out beyond the river flowed past as usual, hiding everything under its calm surface. Here and there the snout of a crocodile head could be seen; the hippos looked around curiously, but all the birds had gone.

It took a bit of time for one to digest this performance, then Juma exclaimed, "Mamba mingi kabissa!" Yes, there truly had been an awful lot of crocodiles, but now they were all in the water, which we would have to cross, and the thought of capsizing was extremely unpleasant. We probably all six harbored the same feelings of apprehension, but nothing was said.

However, the crossing was made without incident. It was now eleven o'clock and we started our journey back. I estimated that we would be back at the elephant village by noon the following day, where I was hoping for good news of more animals with big tusks.

All my love,
Blix

. . . .

Masindi

My darling Cockie,

It is now three weeks since I last wrote you, and during this time I have shot another twenty elephants and believe I have succeeded in driving the herds from this area, which after all was the object of the exercise. Apart from that I have managed to get good tusks on the average, all bulls with the exception of one. This cow, however, gave me a lot of trouble, of which more later on. A couple times the final outcome has looked a bit shaky, but this time of year the terrain is ideal, which makes things a lot easier. If you want to pick out the animal you have chosen in thick forest or in long grass, it takes a lot longer and the risk you take is immeasurably greater. Altogether I have now got 26 elephants with 52 tusks, and I hope and believe that the average will turn out to be about 55 lbs. per tusk, totaling some 2,800 pounds of which half belongs to me at a price of 8 shillings per lb. and so should bring me in over 10,000 shillings. The overhead has been negligible, as I have lived on what is locally obtainable, and porters and other helpers have been paid with meat. The wages for Juma and Abedi are just about the only expense I have had.

But now I have to tell you about the cow I had to shoot. One day when it was raining and I stayed in camp, a couple of excited natives rushed up to me and told me a story of how an irate elephant had killed one of the villagers, who together with a couple of friends had been out in the forest in search of honey. They added that the elephant was absolutely furious and was still standing in a clump of trees only half an hour's walk from my camp. Would I not please come along and kill it? Naturally I was willing to follow, and we set off immediately. The half hour turned out to be nearer two, but this was only to be expected.

When we arrived at the victim's home the village was in turmoil, with the men rattling their newly sharpened spears and the women sitting in a ring on low footstools and howling like moonstruck dogs. They were professional weepers, like the ones you read about in the Bible. They get paid for four days' consecutive weepng when somebody has died, and although it is somewhat macabre it certainly adds to the already prevailing funereal mood. The dead man was still out there; nobody had dared to fetch him. From the village you could see the forest where the tragedy had occurred, a few dozen vultures circling overhead marking the spot.

Juma was with me and also a guide, who carried the heavy .600 which Juma so heartily disliked. A winding path led us to the victim. It turned out to be the same one the honey gatherers had followed that morning. Before we reached the place, two friends of the dead man joined us. They had been cooped up in a tree and had not dared to come down till now. They said the elephant was not far away, still in a rage, trumpeting shrilly and uprooting trees.

We went up to the dead man, whose body had been mutilated to the point where he was hard to identify. The face was relatively intact, however, and I shall never forget the expression of indescribable horror which even after death twisted his features. The ground all around was covered in blood and intestines. The two natives that had succeeded in escaping up the tree had been able to follow the events on the ground and now proceeded to give their account of the happenings. The African story-teller has a great talent for creating an atmosphere of drama and transmitting the feeling of suspense to his audience. These were no exceptions.

Evidently they had just been wandering down the path, studying the treetops for signs of bees nesting. Suddenly, without any warning at all, an angry, trumpeting elephant emerged from the bushes and charged them. The surprised natives scattered in all directions, but just as one of them tried to take cover behind a tree, the elephant reached him with her trunk. The furious animal grabbed him by the waist and speared him repeatedly on one of her tusks—as if he had been a piece of bread, as one of the natives put it. The elephant then banged the dead man against a tree and knelt on him, thereby crushing every bone in his body. After this, she had, wildly trumpeting, kept on aimlessly rushing around pulling up bushes and trees. They finished their narrative by saying they did not think that the elephant was very far away.

I now grabbed the heavy rifle, leaving the Mannlicher with Juma. We left the terrified villagers that had witnessed the massacre, and asked the two most reliable-looking spearmen to come with us. Then we followed the tracks of the elephant, which at first led us in a zigzag direction but eventually straightened out. The spoor was fairly small, so I thought it likely we would have to deal with a cow.

After half an hour's walk we arrived at some droppings, still warm and smoking, so the animal couldn't have been very far away. We gave signs to the spearmen to stay behind and continued ourselves with the utmost caution. We were now in thick forest with dense undergrowth. Not a sound could be heard. Juma went first, foot by foot, searching every bush, every thicket. Just as we arrived in a glade in the forest I happened to break a twig, and the next moment a gray colossus charged us, at the same time emitting deafening trumpet blasts. I fired and jumped to my right at the same time as Juma ran backwards and to the left. It didn't look as if the bullet had had any effect and the animal rushed after Juma with her probing trunk stretched to its limit. As soon as I had recovered my balance, I fired the other barrel towards the vanishing gray monster. A furious trumpeting was heard again, and Juma came rushing back, passing me at a distance of some ten feet with the furious elephant in hot pursuit. The big animal received the bullet in the back of the head and fell with extended neck and all four legs stretched backwards. The distance between the carcass and the last imprint on the ground was more than six feet, so she must have been traveling at a great speed.

Juma came up grinning, "I planned to lead her past you, *Bwana*" written all over his black face. The brave, honest, and unruffled old Juma! The elephant was a cow with long thin tusks, of which the left was still smeared with blood after the gruesome use to which it so recently had been applied. Shreds of human flesh were embedded in the folds around her knees.

We called the spearman by shouting *"Nakufa"* ("She's dead"). Then we collected the fragments of the dead man and put them in a blanket and he was carried to the village on an improvised stretcher. The lamentations from the weepers could be heard from a great distance, but as soon as the news of the marauder's death reached them, their wailings became inter-mingled with shouts of joy at the prospect of feasting and dancing. The blood-stained tusk is still in my possession to remind me of Juma's magnificent self-control as he, with death-defying bravery, led the furious animal past me and so gave me a chance of firing a fatal shot.

With the other elephants I had no trouble, possibly with one exception. One day we were following two bulls and had managed to get up to them twice, but on each occasion they had got our wind and got away. So they knew that they were being hunted, but when they reached a swamp with a very dense growth of palms, they just stayed there, refusing to budge. I don't know if you are familiar with this kind of terrain. It is fairly difficult to describe, but try and picture a hothouse filled with palms and every imaginable leafy plant all joined together by lianas and creepers and you may get an impression of this kind of elephant's paradise.

I crept around on all fours, whilst Juma climbed among lianas, but we could see nothing. In one place, probably no more than ten paces from the nearest elephant, there was a small open space, an old elephant lay-by, which afforded the only chance of a shot. However, it was unlikely that the animals would voluntarily walk into this and I was ready to abandon the chase. Then Juma came up with an idea. I was to remain in the lay-by. He would get out of the palm forest, fix up a couple of torches, approach the elephants from the opposite direction, throw the burning torches at them, and so try to drive them towards the lay-by.

The plan succeeded, but I shall never repeat this procedure! In wild panic the elephants came straight at me. The animal in the lead received a bullet in the head and just before he was on me, checked, turned, and got another bullet in the shoulder. They crashed through the palm thicket like a couple of runaway tanks, leaving in their wake a wide path of overthrown trees and trodden vegetation.

With a triumphant grin on his face, Juma made his way back to where I was standing and we started tracking. There was progressively more and more blood, sprayed from the trunk in all directions, indicating a heart shot. And there he was. Of all the twenty-five bulls, he was the biggest.

Well, now I've been to Michael Moses with my ivory. He was very pleased with the quality and thought the tusks would fetch a good price. The London sale, which will determine the market for all the next quarter, will not take place for another month, but he gave me an advance of 10,000 shillings, so I will have enough for an extended expedition. I am thinking of going to the Belgian Congo in order to familiarize myself with those parts, as well as have a look at the elephants there. One can get a license for four elephants in each district and I think I shall have the time to hunt in four of these. It is all hard ivory there and therefore cheaper, but at the same time the cost of living is less.

All my love,
Blix

. . . .

My darling Cockie,

I had asked Michael Moses to try and get me one of the hundreds of unpopulated islands in Lake Victoria and today I have been out looking at one within easy reach of Jinja. Yesterday I went to that town from here by car and stayed overnight in the charming hotel there. I arrived in time for a quick visit to Ripon Falls. This is where the river starts its long journey to the Mediterranean and is rightly called by Harry Johnson "the birth-place of the Nile." The actual drop is not very high, but the sight of this tremendous volume of water from Lake Victoria gliding in gentle curves like a polished ribbon of steel into the foaming, boiling rapids is really impressive. Hippos were playing and snorting in the lake nearby, and two otters were fishing by the edge of the shore. In the clear water I could see them romping around like seals, coming to the surface, shaking off the water from eyes and whiskers, and taking a cautious look around before diving down again. There were plenty of fish about. I watched them following the gleaming rush of water, I saw them in great shoals in the calm backwaters below the falls, and from there, as at Murchison Falls, they tried in vain to leap the precipitous step up to the lake.

Below the falls several natives were angling with long rods and already had baskets full of fish, mostly a silvery sort of bream, other shot with gold like our carp. Strings of cormorants were flying back and forth over the falls and a few swifts were catching mosquitoes above the curved lines of the surface. Michael Moses had arranged for me to borrow a speedboat to take me to the island, and at seven in the morning it came bubbling up to the landing dock by the hotel. The crew consisted of a small swarthy French mechanic and a native acting as guide. The owner of the boat had gone to Paris, and they were now waiting for a conveyance to send the boat after him, as it was going to be shown at exhibitions in France. The mechanic proudly told me that he had been around the entire Lake Victoria with it, and that this was no mean feat for such a small craft in the turbulent waters often prevailing there.

The luncheon basket, a few bottles of soda water, and a big thermos bottle with ice was brought on board by Abedi. I carried compass and maps and we set off with a roar of powerful engines. Soon we reached twenty-five knots and the Frenchman, who was at the steering wheel, amused himself by passing rocky islets within touching range—demonstrations which I failed to appreciate.

Then we came out in an archipelago of islands and our guide pointed out the one we were looking for, a wooded crescent-shaped islet of about a hundred acres, crowned by a naked cliff about two hundred feet high. One could see white sand on the bank of the creek, and the waves were throwing up foam at the horns of the crescent. While still a distance away I got the feeling that here was paradise. My own island—this had always been my dream! Uninhabited, a beautiful climate, and a lake full of fish. My own boat, no neighbors—but in the middle of this sanctuary also something evil. A giant crocodile was sliding down from a rock, disturbed by the noise from the engines. We slowed down and I went up in the prow to look out for sandbars and sunken rocks. The surface of the small creek was as still and bright as a lagoon and we glided slowly in towards the shore and made fast. The beauty of it all made me gasp for breath. Could it really be true that by paying £10 a year for ninety-nine years I would become the owner of this small paradise?

We went over every yard of the island. On the north side there was a dense wood overgrown with lichen and lianas. The ideal habitat for monkeys and apes, which were not there now, but I was thinking of all those imprisoned behind bars and which I intended to buy and liberate; the vervet monkey and the chimpanzee, my friends. I could already see them there. On the rocky plateau in the center of the crescent there was an open space, very suitable as a house site, and from where a small clear stream flowed into the creek. On one side was a meadow, and there in my imagination I could see every kind of tropical fruit tree, vegetable, berries, and flowers growing in abundance. It would be easy to construct a landing place by a protruding rocky spur in the water.

The woods were teeming with birds—gray and green parrots, weavers, and honey birds. Big hornbills flew with heavy, flapping wings over the treetops, and amongst the dense bush I caught a glimpse of the red tail feathers of the white-crested turaco. Flocks of ducks and teal were floating back and forth in the lagoon and a few crested cranes were grazing in a meadow nearby. Two fish eagles were sitting high up on a dead branch close to the shoreline. Their white heads and necks shone brightly against the dark-blue sky and their pretty brown coats glimmered in the sunlight. Wonderful birds.

A wide path across the meadow indicated that hippos were often there for the grazing, and by the side of the stream we found spoor of water-buck and *sitatunga* [a large antelope with webbed feet, found in swamps, extremely rare]—they must have swum here.

By the turn of the century these islands were thickly populated, cultivated by industrious tribes living on agriculture and fishing. In their well-constructed and strong canoes they were the master of the entire lake (total area more than 26,000 sq. miles) and traveled extensively from island to island. Then came the sleeping sickness, and the only line of action open to the government was to evacuate all the islanders, and, for a period of years, until the disease had disappeared, keep all humans away. Now at last the islands have been declared free from the sickness, and the natives, under strict control, can return to their old homes.

We had our lunch in the cool of the woods and slept away the hottest hours of the day. Then we returned to the boat and made a detour around the neighboring islands. The Frenchman still persisted in going too close to sunken rocks, and whenever I asked him to be cautious I merely got a superior smile in reply, and of course it was his boat and his responsibility. The boat gained speed and we were soon doing twenty-five knots. Suddenly there was a crash and an awful grinding noise and we were all thrown together helter-skelter. Here we were stuck and precariously balanced on top of an underwater rock. As soon as I got to my feet I rushed for a box of matches, which I had stuck in my hat. We were far out in an unpopulated land of islands, and nobody would know where to look for us—only a fire and smoke could show the way. The boat was firmly grounded, with the stern stuck on the underwater obstruction and the bow submerged up to deck level. The Frenchman had turned pale and the natives were trembling with fright. However, it didn't look as if we had sprung a leak, as no water was coming in. Close to the gunwale a big crocodile showed his knobby head and swallowed a fish he had just caught. An unpleasant sight; would we have to swim ashore? The sun was on its way down and in another hour and a half it would be dark. After a few moments of meditation and discussion we decided to all move forward to the bow and thus by shifting the balance of weight get the boat afloat again. Slowly she started to move, and by jumping up and down and rocking her from port to starboard she finally slipped off. Apprehensively, we inspected the hull and to our great relief found no leaks. The self-starter worked—so far everything was fine—the Frenchman cautiously put her in gear, and we started to move forward. Thank God, the propeller was undamaged. What undeserved luck! Soon we were picking up speed and were back in Port Bell before nightfall. I thanked the Frenchman for the trip, got a car to take me to Kampala, and in Michael Moses's beautiful garden I signed the purchase contract for that wonderful island.

All my love,
Blix

. . . .

Butiaba

My darling Cockie,

I am now in Butiaba but intend to cross into the Congo shortly. However, I propose to stay here for a few days as I want to have a look at some
elephants reputed to be found in the lowlands between the Escarpment
and the lake. There are also plenty of buffalo here and the current price
for their hides is high. An Indian in Masindi has promised me £5 and he
would also pay for the transport from Butiaba. I still have Abedi and Juma
with me and in Kampala I provisioned ourselves for a fortnight.

Last night I spent in the governor's camp on the top of the ridge from
where the motor road starts to descend on its winding way down to Lake
Albert. The view from there is beautiful and takes in the entire expanse of
the lake. From the foot of the ridge one can see the road, like a white
ribbon, making its way out to a promontory by the lake shore and there
one gets a glimpse of some houses and a jetty to which a few boats and
barges are moored. There is a boat service to the Belgian ports of Kasenyi
and Mahagi on the other side of the lake and another one up the Nile as
far as Nimule, ninety miles downstream. There the rapids put a stop to
any further traffic by boat and one has to proceed by road. Beyond the
western shore there is a blue-wooded mountain massif and in the clear
morning air one can catch a glimpse of the snow-capped tops of
Ruwenzori. "The Mountains of the Moon" had for a long time defied all
explorers and one had only heard of them through the legends and stories
of the natives. At the foot of these mysterious mountains it was generally
believed the source of the Nile would be found. That this was also the
origin of the impressive basin and complicated Congo river system was
for a long time unknown. It was from there that Baker for the first time in
1862 saw the lake and named it Albert.

A truck took me and my men and the equipment down to Butiaba, where I borrowed an empty house from a government official. In the evening I went out at the request of my host to the tip of the headland to try and shoot some crocodiles that had become a nuisance to the inhabitants. They destroy fishing nets and other equipment and of course consume great quantities of fish. I took the small Mannlicher and found some twenty of the big reptiles lying on the shore. In the cover of a small sand ridge, I managed to get within range. I killed the first one with a bullet in the neck, but at the sound of the shot all the others rushed into the water. After a while they surfaced again, showing just their heads, and I fired at six more, aiming just below the eye. Even if you kill them outright they will sink to the bottom and won't come up for several hours, when gas formed in the abdominal cavity causes them to rise to the surface.

Lake Albert is one of the great reservoirs of the Nile. Most of the enormous volume of water is derived from the Semliki River, which drains the catchment area from the Ruwenzori complex. The eternal snow on the mountaintops and the heavy rainfall in this region makes the in-flow high and steady. In addition there are many lesser sources from the highlands between Kasenyi and Mahagi. In the north the lake narrows into a funnel and there the Victoria Nile discharges its waters. Copernicus already wrote about the Mountains of the Moon and about two lakes that were mothers to the widely known Nile River. This matter of the source of the Nile has been the subject and speculation of innumerable storytellers from time immemorial, and it was only when Speke arrived at Lake Victoria in 1861 and Baker came to Lake Albert a year later that the true facts became known.

The whole of this area is to some degree awe-inspiring. Everything is now the same as it has always been—the only differences being that one now finds constructed motor roads and that there are rivercraft manned and owned by white people. The native's way of life is the same; he lives in the same sort of hut, eats the same food. Elephant, buffalo, and hippopotamus tread the same paths, the crocodile fishes in the same waters—as undisturbed now as they were then. Will the progress of civilization during the future generations destroy all this? Will the white man drive out the black man, or vice versa? Will modern science find cures for many pests and diseases which are now rampant among man and beast? Will the many cheap means of transport of today and tomorrow make an exploitation of these vast and fertile areas possible?

Millions of acres of now uninhabited fertile land would then be able to produce coffee, tea, maize, sisal, simsim oil, livestock, and so butter, cheese, and frozen meat—more than enough to feed the overpopulated parts of the world. These big lakes are teeming with fish and when in the evenings you sit by the shore it looks as if the surface is boiling. When Emin Pasha was cut off from the outside world by the Mahdist uprising and the Senussi's victory over General Gordon, it was here that he was forced to create his own independent state. However, when Stanley in 1887 succeeded in getting here, through the primeval forests of the Congo, in order to rescue him—he refused to be rescued. How well I understand him!

From the village the beat of the drums can be heard, the hippos are blowing and panting down by the lake, in the mountain ravines the lions are serenading, the crickets and bullfrogs are filling the air with noise, and clouds of mosquitoes dance to their own music.

Butiaba and the surrounding area is certainly no health resort. Malaria is rife everywhere, as is black-water fever, and sleeping sickness has depopulated entire districts. The natives look to be in a bad condition, with nasty sores that never seem to heal. The need for more hospitals and medical aid is increasing all the time. I have given mosquito nets and clothing to all my employees and force them to take quinine every day.

I have been out for two days, hunting between the highlands and the lake. There is a lot of game here. Big herds of Uganda cob, waterbuck, and Jackson's hartebeest. I have seen smaller herds of buffalo and here and there some elephants. I spent one night by a stream some twenty miles north of here under some tall palm trees. The sighing in the fronds from the gentle night breeze sounded like the lapping of waves against a shore. A family of lions roared all night in a dry riverbed nearby, a leopard coughed further down towards the lake, and the hyenas howled all around the nearest village. The moon was up and the stars twinkled in a clear sky.

The next morning I went out to look for lion, as I had promised Michael Moses a couple of skins. Before dawn I was on my way towards the place where I had heard them during the night. They often keep up their serenading till well after sunrise. The sound would give you an indication of direction and sometimes they could be found in front of some thicket or stretched out on a flat piece of rock, sunning themselves, before seeking cover and shade in a clump of bushes or some crevice.

This is also how it came to pass. Just as the sky in the east was beginning to redden and a tiara of golden rays announced the arrival of the sun, the lions struck up a hymn, greeting the dawn in unison. I could make out at least three different voices. It is difficult to estimate distance from these vibrating roars, but I got the general direction and so we set off as fast as we could without making too much noise—Juma, myself, and a local native. Perhaps they would give another greeting to the new day—or say good-bye to the night. The sun rose like a glowing ball over the ridge and one could already feel its warmth.

Suddenly we heard a hollow *uh-uh* quite close. They seemed to be behind a bank of thick undergrowth about a hundred yards away. We approached as quietly as possible. To the right was a narrow opening in the bushes, with a cliff on one side, and we crawled forward in that direction. Maybe we would be able to see them from there. Another *uh-uh, uh-uh*. They were evidently awake. I wasn't wearing sneakers or moccasins, just ordinary shoes, and by the foot of the cliff I took them off and continued barefoot—the last bit inch by inch. And there they were, lying on a patch of grass in front of the bushes: two males, a lioness, and two half-grown cubs. One of the lions had a good mane, dark turning to black around the ears, more golden-brown by the shoulders. They were magnificent. The young ones played and rolled about in the usual feline manner. I sat watching them for a long time before I made a whistling sound, and they all jumped up and stood for a moment listening. Before they had time to rush off, I fired at the best one, aiming at the shoulder, and then, as if by magic, they all disappeared into the thick undergrowth. I was sure I had hit him, as he had emitted a short grunt as the bullet struck. We waited for a short while where we stood and then slowly went forward. A few drops of blood glistened on the green grass. We made a detour around the scrub but could see no spoor leading out of it. I was standing, thinking about our best course of action, when the lioness, her eyes smoldering, fangs bared, and accompanied by the sound of a fearful roar and the crash of broken twigs, came at us as if shot out of a catapult. She received the small bullet in the forehead and, propelled by her own speed, made a complete somersault. The whole thing was over so quickly that it almost defies description.

We stood for quite a while, myself with the rifle at the ready, wondering if any of the others would attack, but not a sound was heard. We threw some stones and lumps of earth into the thicket, but there was no reaction. It only remained to follow the blood-spoor. I went in followed by Juma, who carefully inspected every bush. Suddenly he froze and pointed. A patch of yellow could be dimly seen between the branches; I whistled but nothing moved. Juma threw a stone—still nothing—and we went on. There he was, stone-dead, and no sign of the others. The sun was well up by then and we sent for our followers to come and help with the skinning and the transport, and then we went back for a rest and a meal.

In the afternoon, news came in about buffalo a good day's march from here up towards the northern part of the lake. As I had thought of remaining here for another couple of days, I sent for the headman of the village and let him know that if he, by the following day, could supply porters to carry back the hides of any buffalo shot, he and his villagers would get all the meat. This he promised to do, and I started to sort out my provisions and equipment for a four-day safari. Just bed clothing, mosquito net, potatoes, rice, pepper, salt, sugar, and tea—eggs I would get from the natives, and meat and fish on the way.

The fishermen had found four dead crocodiles from yesterday's hunt, and later in the afternoon I went out on the sandspit and shot one on land and four in the water. I bought a splendid freshly caught Nile perch, which Abedi prepared for my dinner like we do cod at home, with potatoes, melted butter, and chopped hard-boiled eggs. From the village I got news that fifty men had volunteered to come with me on the safari, twelve from here and the rest from another village further up towards the mountains. I would have to provision them with maize meal, two lbs. per man per day, which meant some thirty loads. In addition, I bought three loads of coarse salt for the curing of the hides.

All my love,
Blix

My darling Cockie,

My four-day safari is completed. I am now sitting writing this by the light of the lamp, tired and satisfied and with a whisky and soda by my side while millions of mosquitoes are threading their eternal dance outside the tent. The moon is full and his yellow face is reflected on the bright surface of Lake Albert. Every now and then the top layers of the water are broken by a fish jumping and then falling back again with a splash. There is a faint rustle from the raffia palms when the sleepy night breeze passes through their fronds. There is dancing in the village and I can hear the beat of the drums. In the light of the full moon a great proportion of the millions living on the African continent dance every night without restrictions, without thoughts other than gladness and the joy of living—like the dance of the mosquitoes at dusk, like the fishes in the water, like the birds in the sky. Can we improve on this?

I was both lucky and unlucky on this safari. I got, all told, twelve buffalo—all bulls—and that wasn't bad, but I was unfortunate with a big elephant who got disturbed by the sound of gunfire and went up towards the mountains and into the game reserve. He really had colossal tusks, and I could follow his zigzagging way up the slopes.

The second day I had my best hunt. By a stream where the buffalo had been grazing during the night I found the spoor of six bulls, and for once they were walking against a prevailing wind blowing steadily from the north. We followed this spoor for two hours through open bush country and finally came to an isolated clump of trees, from which a small brook emanated. The foot of the mountain range was now only half a mile away to the east, and in the west the terrain was completely open, a wide expanse of meadowland dotted with antheaps and isolated palm trees. In the north, two hundred yards of flat ground bare of vegetation and beyond that the country became wooded. As far as I could see, the buffalo, if disturbed, would make their way from the copse towards me in order to reach the nearest shelter. I took it for granted that they would not in this heat start climbing into the high country above them.

After a few minutes' palaver it was decided that Juma and I should position ourselves at the northeastern side of the copse, that four men should go out onto the plains with the palm trees to stop the animals from breaking out there, and that the rest should follow the tracks.

Soon we heard the sound of galloping hooves and the breaking of twigs. Then they stopped, listening for a couple of minutes, some bellowing, and off they went again. Having reached the open patch of grassland, they stopped. The range was no more than sixty yards, but I didn't want to fire, as they might turn back. With necks fully stretched and heads raised, they were surveying the terrain whilst their attendants, the white cattle egrets, anxiously fluttered around them. The scenery was magnificent.

When they again broke into a gallop, I hurriedly fired at the two hindmost animals, both of them registering hits. Juma handed me the Mannlicher, and with a bullet to the neck the leading bull fell to the ground. The others checked and then turned about, galloping back in their own tracks. The two that had first been fired at stopped on tottering legs, and the remaining three came thundering straight at me. Juma handed me the double-barreled rifle, which he had by now reloaded, and the leading one got a bullet in the chest, the second one swerved and I fired, aiming at the shoulder, before he reached the shelter of the woods. Then he disappeared with a crash.

The two leading ones had fallen, and now there were within a two-hundred-yard radius five dead buffalo bulls. The natives were jubilant and were crowding together around the fallen animals—five big bulls and tons of meat! Word was sent for women with knives, pots, baskets, and beer brewed from honey, as all this was going to take some time.

Juma and I went after the last bull, who had entered the woods. I knew that the bullets had found the right spot, and soon we found plenty of blood. As you know, a wounded buffalo frequently backtracks and positions himself a few yards to one side in readiness to attack a pursuing enemy—whether he is a lion, a spear-carrying native, or a white man with a firearm. One has to proceed with the utmost caution, watching every bush, every piece of scrub.

Juma suddenly caught my arm and pointed. There, to my left, the buffalo was standing; I could only see the drooping tail. At that moment I happened to tread on a dried-out twig and, like an avalanche, he was on us. At a distance of a few yards I got a glimpse of his gleaming black horns and aimed at the spot a foot below them; with a broken neck he fell at our feet.

It was difficult to keep the natives reasonably quiet and to dampen their enthusiasm, in order not to disturb the game in the vicinity.

Still, it was one of the more exciting hunts I had experienced. The first day I had got three bulls, the second six, the third one, and the last two—twelve in all. The hides, lightly salted, I sent by truck to an Indian in Masindi who had promised me 100 shillings apiece, so with this small safari I had made 1,200 shillings.

With today's mail from Nairobi I received a letter from Jeff Manley [Blix's manager], who wrote that there had been an inquiry from a Englishman whether I would be willing to take him and his wife out on a hunting safari in this area. This would suit me admirably, partly because I would get to know the district better at their expense, and partly because I would receive £200 in cash. It would also mean a pleasant break in one's solitude. I therefore sent an affirmative reply by telegram and also gave instructions about equipment, time and place for rendezvous, et cetera.

I am planning to stay here for another few days to do some fishing in case this amuses them, and then will take a boat up to Rhino Camp in order to hunt along the Nile and then carry on towards the Sudan border by the Aswa River. There is supposed to be plenty of game in this area, elephant, buffalo, and white rhino (wrongly named, as the squared-nose species has the same coloring as the ordinary black one), masses of hippo, crocodile, lion, Uganda cob, kongoni, waterbuck, and much more. The terrain is very suitable for photography and right now the grass is green and not too long.

All my love,
Blix

CHAPTER

6

• •

Rhino Camp

My darling Cockie,

Again some time has passed since I last wrote you, but I have had a lot of things to do for the Markhams,* and I am pleased to say that we get on very well together.

At first we did some fishing close to Butiaba and took a few minor safaris along the shores. They liked Lake Albert very much. The water is so blue and the surrounding mountains vary in many different colors. Pleasing slopes alternate with dark green ravines where foaming streams dropping over the blue massif of the impressive Ruwenzori Mountains can be seen.

In the mornings Charles Markham very much enjoyed catching tiger-fish with rod and line. The average weight is about one pound and they put up a good fight. Late in the afternoons we then used the meat as bait when we went out in rowing boats to fish for Nile perch on a drag line. We didn't manage to get a really big one, but we got two of about twenty-five lbs. and one of these fought for fully forty-five minutes. What a marvelous fish for the dinner table, poached with melted butter and new potatoes. One felt just as though it were being served in Krogs Fish Restaurant by Gammelstrand in Copenhagen.

We lived on the 175-ton lake streamer *Samuel Baker* and life on board was fairly comfortable. She was supposed to have gone into dock for an overhaul, but we managed to get this postponed and, for a reasonable sum, were able to charter her for a week.

Gwladys Markham was mostly interested in bathing and catching but-

---

*Sir Charles Markham later became a very great friend of Blix's, and it was with him he undertook the first crossing of the Sahara with a four-wheeled vehicle (in 1928). Lady Markham later became Lady Delamere (mayor of Nairobi).

terflies. Swimming in these crocodile-infested waters is not a pastime to be recommended, still we managed to find a shallow sandy beach and whilst the lady was splashing around Charles and I stood guard with loaded rifles. After four days in Butiaba, we took the *Samuel Baker* up to Murchison Falls, a wonderful trip up the Victoria Nile. We saw a tremendous amount of game along the banks: grazing and bathing elephant, herds of buffalo, masses of Uganda cob and waterbuck, and in the river hundreds of hippo showing their shapeless heads, twitching their short ears, blowing and snorting. Once when we were near land, one of them happened to come between the boat and the bank. It was too shallow for him to dive, and instead he tried to out-distance us but could just manage to keep pace. He gained a bit as long as he could splash along in the shallows, but lost it whenever he got into a hole in the river bottom. He was clumsy, fantastic, unreal, as he rushed forward in his frightened eagerness. A bit further on the boat swerved and he managed to get past. Poor fellow, he got a shock, but we a good laugh and many yards of film.

On the sandspit and all along the banks were masses of crocodiles diving into the water with terrific splashes as the boat approached. On one occasion only one remained on the bank, evidently not worrying about our presence even though the crew whistled and shouted at him. Only when he was hit by a potato on his back did he, startled out of his sleep, take any notice and remove himself into the safety of the river. He was probably old and deaf, like so many of us humans.

We anchored in "the great entrance" which I have previously described and had a delightful evening in the mosquito-proof and comfortable dining room on the upper deck of the boat. We sat there in the light of the tropical moon overwhelmed by the roar from the falls, which the whole time varied in pitch and intensity in accordance with the direction of the breeze. We listened to the monotonous hum from the insects and all the other enchanting sounds from the wilds: the hoofed animals' peculiar thud, the hippos' blowing, and the lions' serenading in the distance. The round yellow moon hung clearer and friendlier than anywhere else. No disturbing noises from humans, no dogs barking, no drumbeats. Nature such as it is, and has been, for thousands of years.

Next day we returned to Lake Albert and then proceeded northwards along the papyrus swamp and into the wide, calm, and majestic White Nile. Clusters of green water lilies were floating on top of tiny wavelets stirred by the faint morning breeze. The deck was still wet from the dew, the air was cool and clear, and fish were jumping boisterously high above the yellow water. The heat had as yet not put its oppressive stamp on the surroundings.

We zigzagged down the river. The native helmsman was familiar with every sandbar and underwater hazard. We slowed down whenever the water became shallow and one man attended to the sounding line in a calm and efficient manner. All day long we glided along the papyrus. Here and there a lone tree broke the monotony of the line of reeds. The birdlife was rich and varied: herons, egrets, geese, duck, weaver birds, black shrikes, white spoonbills, and different species of ibis, et cetera.

By four o'clock we arived at Rhino Camp. The district commissioner had put a uniformed *askari** at our disposal, and fifty native porters were paraded in two ranks with the local headman out in front—all as God had made them, completely naked. The village chief was gracefully reclining in an armchair of European pattern, and behind him he had his two favorite wives in attendance. Further back were small boys carrying live chickens tied up in pairs by their legs with heads hanging down (the usual way of transporting poultry in Africa), as well as beautifully plaited baskets filled with eggs, ground nuts, sweet potatoes, bananas, and pineapples. There were also rows of maize cobs, maniock root, pumpkins, and dry, smoked fish, so it didn't look as if we were going to starve! Numerous drums and large quantities of firewood indicated a disturbed night ahead with prolonged dancing.

It was by then too late to send the boat back, so we decided to spend the night on board and make camp the following morning. We had good reports about game: herds of elephant by the swamps quite close to the Nile, and rhinos not far from there. As you know, it is here on the west bank of the river we had "the white rhino"—the black one has never crossed the Nile. The white species is somewhat bigger, has a more drawn-out head, and carries bigger horns. In contrast to his black brother, he is a much more peaceful animal and becomes aggressive only on very rare occasions. He is also now protected in all districts where he can be found.

Our first days of hunting were quite extraordinary. We got no less than six elephants, two rhinos, four hippos, and two lions, apart from Uganda cob and waterbuck with good heads. What impressed me most was our meeting with the elephants not more than three miles from our camp, out in open grassland, by the river. Here and there big sheets of water were

---

*Swahili for policeman, guard, or soldier.

still remaining after the big rains three weeks earlier. Already in the distance we could see big flocks of cattle egrets flying in the direction of the plains, whereby we understood that there must be elephants there. The birds follow these, catching insects that swarm around them or picking ticks from their thick hides. They are welcome guests and ride jauntily on the broad backs of their hosts.

The country was flat, with only gently rising ground and occasional shallow depressions, the monotony being broken by isolated trees and antheaps. We sent a boy up in a tree to observe and he shouted down that there were masses of elephant in the distance. During the rains the animals had been wandering around there and the now-hardened imprints in the clay were a foot deep and made our progress towards the herd very tiring. It was already hot in spite of the fact that the sun was still low on the horizon.

From a tall antheap we soon got our first view of the elephants—a dense mass of gray backs with a leading edge of about half a mile. On the fringes of the herd were smaller groups of animals, with here and there a solitary bull. What would now be the best plan? The wind was right—an even southerly breeze was blowing from the elephants towards us. It was important not to be too hasty; it was not impossible that one of the biggest beasts, with the biggest tusks, was hiding somewhere within the herd! I sent out two scouts to have a look at the bulls that were standing by themselves close to the river, whilst we ourselves approached the main concentration of animals.

When we were about four hundreds yards away, we made a halt in order to survey the animals through the field glasses. One got a clear view of those that were standing on the fringes, although they occasionally changed positions, but generally there was no great movement within the herd as they were obviously enjoying their siesta. Their enormous ears were idly flapping, now and then a probing trunk was raised, or a shrill trumpet call came from a mother rebuking an obstreperous calf, or a young miss a bachelor being too fresh.

It was an impressive sight. In this comparatively small area there were four to five hundred elephants. I couldn't help thinking back to the days when Walter Bell (or Karamoja Bell as he was known) was the first to disturb these herds, all of which he so realistically recounts in his book *The Wanderings of an Elephant Hunter.* This was the area that was called the Lado Enclave and which was leased to King Leopold of Belgium for the duration of his life, after he had acquired the rights to what is now the

Belgian Congo, but which at that time was a somewhat imaginary concep-
tion, taking in the Congo River basin. Bell happened to arrive here just as
the lease expired with the death of King Leopold and before the British
Government had incorporated the district within the Uganda Protector-
ate. In the interim period, hunting became a free-for-all, and I would
think that Bell then shot more elephants than anybody else had done, or
will ever do, in such a short time.

From our lookout we couldn't see any big bulls, but after a short while
our two scouts returned telling us that there were four big bulls standing
by themselves down by the river, and of these two carried big ivory.

I then detailed two boys out to the right and told them to climb a big
thorn tree and from there observe any big bull that happened to be con-
tained in the herd, and to keep an eye on them should the whole lot move
off.

It was now beginning to get warm, and Lady Markham was suffering
from the heat a bit. However, I didn't dare leave her behind, as one never
knew how elephants would react. It is never very safe to run away from
them, in case they come straight at you, but we all knew we would have a
strenuous day, so she had better come with us.

After a quarter of an hour's walk we got the four bulls within sight and I
estimated the weight of their respective tusks as being ninety, eighty, and
two at forty-five lbs. Between us and the animals there was only one fairly
small antheap to use as a hiding place, and from there it was only fifty
yards to our target, and so we crawled forward in single file, with myself first, then the Markhams, and behind them Juma and two natives
with second guns. Charles and I had a .450 each and Gwladys a light
Mannlicher.

The bulls were sleepy, standing slowly flapping their ears and occasionally smacking them against their sides. Still half asleep, they sucked up
loose topsoil from the earth which they had scraped up with their forefeet
and sprayed it over their necks and backs.

Step by step, we crept forward. You know how very exciting it is. As
many as we were, it could easily happen that one might sneeze or stum-
ble, and all would be lost. Luckily, there were no alert egrets on their
backs.

Now we had reached the antheap. Charles was very keyed up—I
thought I could almost hear his heartbeats. "Take it easy, we have plenty
of time." Slowly, we squatted in the grass and observed the animals. How
terribly big an elephant is at close quarters—like an enormous gray wall.

Naturally the biggest was standing furthest away—but there was a clear line of fire to his head, and the second one was just behind him with his head level with the flank of the one in front.

We decided that Gwladys would have the first shot and should aim at the head of the biggest. In case it didn't fall I would fire a second round at it, and at the same time Charles would shoot at the second, aiming at the shoulder. The two lesser ones were turned towards us, and it was impossible to foresee which way they would move. Gwladys was able to rest her rifle on the antheap, and I asked her to take it easy, completely unnecessarily as it turned out, as she was the calmest of us all. I was to the right of her, and Charles and Juma on the other side of the antheap.

In situations like this, moments take hours to pass and one expects a shot and further developments, in what direction it's impossible to guess. A mosquito stung me in the forehead, but I didn't dare chase it away as I was expecting action at any moment. Then the second elephant took an unexpected step forward, thereby screening off the big one from view. The chance had gone—but the day was yet young. The moment's tension had passed and we all exhaled. Maybe it was best this way—calmer nerves give steadier hands.

We sat for ten minutes quietly and silently waiting. Presently the elephants woke up from their half slumber, moved about a bit, and then slowly sort of floated out in single file with the biggest in the lead, but still very hesitantly. I nodded to Gwladys; the rest of us had our firearms at the ready. Calmly she raised her rifle, aimed, and squeezed the trigger. The hind legs of the big bull folded and he slowly toppled to the ground, all life extinct. His pals went into a huddle with their trunks in the air; then came Charles' shot, then another one, and then they rushed off in the direction of the herd. I fired at the shoulder of the wounded one from diagonally behind, but he continued on his way, keeping up with the rest. After a few hundred yards he started to fall behind, but managed to get up to the herd, where he disappeared. This big gray mass was now thoroughly alert. Trunks were raised and there was some angry and shrill trumpeting.

We had a look at the fallen bull and then approached the herd. A good animal threw his head up, exhibiting a fine pair of tusks—possibly he would emerge from among the rest. We didn't dare get any nearer than a hundred yards, as one didn't know what they were going to do. We were now between the elephants and the papyrus by the river. Were they going to seek shelter here or wander off towards the bush country about a mile away? The answer was neither. They just stood there—a colossal gray wall.

We parked ourselves on some tussocks and waited for an hour without anything happening. The egrets had flown away and the sun was high in the sky, causing trembling heat waves. In the far distance one could just make out the dim contours of a few antelopes; the animals appeared to be hanging in the air, almost a mirage. Above us vultures and marabou storks were soaring in wide circles; they had long ago discovered the dead elephant.

I called the two boys that were sitting in the thorn trees and told them to go around on the windward side of the herd and to there light a fire. Smoke and the scent from humans might possibly make them move. The answer to this maneuver, however, was negative. The heat was by then becoming unbearable, and we decided to go back to camp, leaving four men behind. Even here, in the shade, it was hot, but Abedi had pitched the tents, the lunch was ready, and under a spreading tree stood the mess tent, complete with mosquito net and camp chairs.

The men came back at two o'clock with the news that the herd had started trekking up towards the mountains and that the second elephant was dead. Charles and I went out to have a look. We estimated the weight of the biggest pair of tusks to be about ninety lbs. each, the lesser sixty lbs. On board the boat we had taken a thirty-hundredweight lorry, which Manley had sent up from Nairobi together with the tentage. This was the first motor vehicle ever seen here, and the natives were naturally completely overwhelmed with surprise and curiosity at such a sight. I had heard in Butiaba that it was possible to drive from here to Arua. This is where my old friend the district commissioner, Charles Bruton, resides and he could surely give us good advice and recommendations.

It proved to be an eventful night. In this district there hadn't been so much meat in one place at one time for a very long time, and it had to be celebrated. The dancing and singing could be heard over a very wide area, and the bush telegraph spread the glad news from village to village. The next morning, just as we were about to depart for Arua in our vehicle, news came in that two big elephants were standing by the river just north of the camp. Such an opportunity could not be missed. Gwladys did not feel like another longish walk in the heat and elected to stay in camp, so Charles and I went off on our own. However, the elephants only carried small ivory, so we let them go. As we were carrying food and water with us, we decided to make a detour on our way back. We came upon a quite good bull, which Charles shot, and he also got a couple of antelope.

I am not going to tire you with a description of the other day's hunting. However, you should have been with us on the trip to Arua. It became quite a sensation—"The boat is traveling on land" is what the natives shouted at our approach and they tried to follow us as fast as their legs could carry them.

Bruton himself looked somewhat astonished when he saw us swinging up in front of the entrance to his small stone residence. Arua is a picturesque little outpost. Bruton and his assistant live in one bungalow. Then there is an office building, a dispensary and medical officer's quarters, a mission house and school, and, a short distance away, the trading village, with some ten Indian shops where you can buy anything from beads to hides to bicycles.

Within the district, which included everything under British flag on this side of the Nile, cotton, grain, mostly maize, and millet is produced. In some parts there are plenty of cattle and sheep, and the indigenous population works hard and lives well. The sleeping sickness, however, remains a scourge, and the work of medical officers is by no means easy.

All my love,
Blix

· ·

Butiaba

My darling Cockie,

Now we are back again in Butiaba after a pleasant trip through some, in many ways, beautiful country which you can find in the west Nile district. The terrain is fairly flat interspersed with isolated hills, which, when standing out against the horizon, assist in giving direction.

We have seen a lot of buffalo and shot a few for the pot. All have been of the Sudan species, which is smaller than the Uganda buffalo. What I have been particularly interested in is the discovery of a herd of eland antelopes which I found close to the Kaja River almost on the boundary of the Sudan. These must have been Lord Derby's eland, also called Giant Eland, but as far as I know never previously having been found and shot in this area. Stupidly enough I did not shoot one at the time, as it did not dawn on me until too late that they might be of this species. A herd of some thirty animals trotted quite calmly past me at a distance of a hundred and fifty yards. The other side of the Kaja River is Sudanese territory and also a game reserve, which means the wild life is completely undisturbed.

We saw quite a lot of white rhino, and as I had been asked by the game warden in Kampala to try and make an estimate of the number of this family in the district, I spent a considerable time doing just this. The Markhams had licenses to shoot one each, and they both got good bulls, their horns measuring thirty-two and thirty-three inches respectively.

I once came upon a track of a bull which showed up in the most peculiar zigzag pattern. At first I thought he must have been dragging a branch along on which he had been chewing. But when I had been following the spoor for a quarter of an hour and the same pattern repeated, I started to wonder whether my theory had been correct and decided to carry on in order to find out the reason for this peculiarity. I had Juma and two other natives with me.

After two hours of tracking we caught up to the bull where he was standing sleeping under a tree. The white rhino has, as I've mentioned previously, a longish head and the front horn does not, like his black cousins', point straight up, but rather obliquely forward. This bull had a fantastically long horn and the upper part was pointing downwards. Here was the answer to what had caused the zigzag line in the spoor. It was a pity I did not have the camera with me. Close to the tree there was a puddle of water where he had rolled and had a good wallow and in the mud I found an imprint of his whole body and was able to measure the length of the horn—42.5 inches!

One morning when we were out gathering mushrooms, we came across two fresh spoor of lion in the dewy grass. We had our rifles with us and Markham's gunbearer started tracking. After half an hour the dew evaporated and the spoor became difficult to follow. We stopped for a while in order to consider what best to do. The tracker thought that the lion had gone to the right, whilst I was convinced the tracks were bearing left. Markham smiled and said he would follow his tracker. I took Lady Markham and Juma with me, and we set off with myself in the lead.

The only signs we had to go by were a few slightly bent blades of grass and the occasional small stone which had been dislodged by the animals, and we could only proceed at a snail's pace.

At the foot of an antheap we found a place where the lions had been resting and the ground was still warm from their bodies. We were obviously on the right track! Juma discarded his sandals (we had crepe soles) and step by step we followed the faint pugmarks, now completely alert. We breathed deeply and quietly. Have you also noticed that tension makes one's intake of air more strained—especially when one is continuously listening and does not even dare to blink!

Just ahead of us I could see something white and pointed it out to Gwladys, who, being somewhat shorter than myself, however, was unable to spot it. What could it be? I managed to climb a flat piece of rock and saw a sleeping lion with his back towards us. The white coloring I had first noticed was the skin of his distended belly—the evening's meal must have been adequate. Silently, I gave Lady Markham a helping hand in mounting the boulder. Now we could clearly see his impressive mane and black ears. I indicated the target area by pointing my finger towards Lady Markham's neck, and she slowly raised her Mannlicher. "Take it easy, we have plenty of time!" She smiled and pressed the trigger. All four legs straightened out at once; the spinal column had been broken and he was very dead.

Startled out of his sleep, number two woke up with a roar. He approached us obliquely but had as yet not spotted us. The first shot was a miss, the second got him, and for my supporting bullet he rolled over. Even this one was a good lion, but with a somewhat lighter mane.

There was quiet jubilation, with all the camp followers rushing up and Lady Markham being carried back in triumph on the shoulders of four powerful natives at the head of a procession which included the dead lions.

Now we are in Butiaba again and the Markhams have decided to remain here for another few days as they wish to amuse themselves with fishing and crocodile hunting. I am going to make preparations for a trip into the interior of the Ituri Forest. I very much want to at least catch sight of an okapi—I don't think it will be possible now to obtain a license for shooting one. I am going to take very little with me—my big rifle and a .22, Juma and Abedi, some cooking pots, blankets, a sleeping bag, and two light one-man tents. It is going to be a cheap and easily managed safari. I'll write to you, but the mail will now take longer, as it will have to be posted at Boma. If I only had you with me!

All my love
Blix

CHAPTER
7

My dear Dick,

The flames from the campfire illuminate the treetops of the rain forest in a whirling display and the lianas seem to come to life like snakes gliding between branches and leaves. Sparks are lit, dance, and die, and the whitish-yellow smoke gyrates up towards the dark foliage. Round the boiling pots, women and children are squatting, sniffing the meat-rich fragrance from the filled vessels. It's a peaceful atmosphere after a hard day.

I have now been here west of Ituri by the river Nepoko for three weeks. I have the least possible amount of equipment with me and am now sitting writing by the light from a hurricane lamp whilst my hosts are having their evening meal. They form a small part of the Wambuti tribe, pygmies, the original inhabitants but now to some extent been made to succumb to foreign rule.

I have lived with them, tried to understand them and gain their confidence, but I don't think I have succeeded. I believe they regard me as one not being quite right in his head, and perhaps I have the same idea about them. Still, we are great friends and I have provided meat for them— monkeys are a great delicacy, possibly because they are difficult to bring down with primitive weapons. From other natives I have procured bananas and I have given them as much salt as they have required.

I don't really know whether they really are frightened of me or not. I don't think they are, although they say that a white man is as scary as a ghost is to us. They cannot, of course, understand why we live as we do and not as they do. To follow a white man is for them confusing and exasperating. He is unable, like them, to proceed swiftly and soundlessly in difficult terrain, nor can he—dry-shod—cross a water obstacle by swinging from liana to liana. He is unable to rob the wild bees of their honey, he is unable to catch the young from the gray parrots, he is unable to harvest the fruit clusters of the palm trees growing thirty yards up. He doesn't know which are the best roots to cook with his meat, nor the best way to prepare the rattan in order to make it soft and pliable over the fire. He doesn't know the different dyes in the bark of the trees, he doesn't know how to set up a mouse snare, and even less how to prepare the result in an appetizing way. No, the white man doesn't know very much, and mostly he is a great nuisance. However, he provides salt, shoots monkeys, and maybe, just possibly, he can kill an elephant, as he has said he can.

Yes, it looks as if I soon will have to, unless I'm going to lose all prestige—but those I've seen so far haven't been worth shooting. Nevertheless, there ought to be good ivory, as nobody has previously hunted here for that commodity—only for meat, which of course is the great problem in this primeval forest where there is no pasture. The natives have been forbidden to wage war against each other, consequently there are no prisoners or casualties—and so no meat. What, really, is the white man thinking of—how is he going to solve this question of meat?

We speak the same language, these pygmies and myself. It is rather like communicating with animals, and I don't mean this in any derogatory way. A hunter has a tremendous lot to learn from them. They follow tracks where no tracks are visible, they share the thoughts of their quarry, and know all their habits and times inside out.

To move through the forest without a sound is for them the easiest thing in the world, for me an impossibility, a fact they have known for a long time. Soon, I believe they will give up all hope and leave me. In order to tempt them to stay longer, I have promised to shoot them an elephant. In case he should have poor ivory, we have agreed to keep our mouths shut—keep quiet and eat. I only have a license for five elephants in this district and can't afford small tusks.

Now my small friends have finished eating. Tremendous belches, unbelievable from such small frames, announce that their dinner has been satisfactory. A shrill boy's voice strikes the first note, then a hand bangs on the taut skin of the drum. All get together and make a ring. All know the same melody, the same rhythm. Small feet stamp hard and in time, heads swing, and behinds move. Enjoyment, the simple, untroubled, natural enjoyment, reigns supreme. Here there are no restrictions, no danceless days—except when the tropical rain comes pelting down!

The forest here is very beautiful and the spring has set in, i.e., the rains have started. This morning I crossed a riverbed with wide swamplike banks covered in big chalk-white lilies with a wonderful scent. The straight light-colored trunks of the mahogany tree shoot proudly up in the air and between them are palm trees of various kinds as well as broad-leafed wild bananas, which, however, don't yield any fruit. The rattan stems snake right up to the top of the trees, where they spread out in pretty palmlike fronds. White orchids adorn branches and twigs, mosses in different shades spread out between the bracken, and various types of grasses and other leafy plants luxuriate as if they were in a giant green-house. I have counted up to eleven different species of monkey and ape, from a tiny red-brown fellow with a white tip of the nose to the black chimpanzees. Hornbills fly with heavy, cumbersome wings from tree to tree and there are great flocks of gray parrots whistling melodiously as they fly to and fro. The scenery is in many ways similar to Uganda, but somehow one feels the wilderness more intensely here. Thanks to my little friends and in spite of my own clumsiness I've had the luck of seeing no less than seven okapi antelopes. I am not allowed to shoot any, nor do I dare to, although the pygmies assure me they would have finished all vestiges of the carcass long before any government official could have arrived on the scene. For a European it is looked upon as a major breach of the law to kill an okapi, whilst the native may eat them as often as he gets the chance.

It was early one morning when I saw the first ones. They came from the forest to seek shelter and rest for the day on a small hillock overgrown with high grass and leafy plants ten to twelve feet tall standing as close together as reeds. In there not even a Wambuti or the most supple panther could have moved without sound. I sat motionless with my pygmy, and as luck would have it—or was it because of his inexplicable instinct?—we were in the right place at the right time. They came at the trot with stretched necks and long strides, splashing and making noises like elk when crossing a small watercourse very close by. They appeared to be almost black, with lighter heads, and the pretty white stripes on their shoulders and hindquarters stood out clearly in the half-light of the for-est. It was a magnificent sight, which I was experiencing for the first time, and which so very few white men have ever seen.

Another evening I saw two more inside the forest. They came slowly towards me and moved like gerenuks, carrying their heads low and necks stretched, carefully probing the ground as they slid under branches and lianas. They were big dark bulls. When they were about thirty feet away they got my wind, immediately turned about, and, like two bolting horses, rushed down through the valley and disappeared on the other side.

One hot afternoon, I came upon another two in dense undergrowth. This time I just got a glimpse of black animals and kicking legs as they dived into the scrub. One day I may get a license to shoot one for some museum—but just to see one is an unforgettable sensation in itself.

Now the dancing is in full swing, and spirits run high. Juma and Abedi, who have been able to acquire a girl each, take a vigorous part in the proceedings, singing and swaying like the best of them. No sorrows or cares here, no gossip or quarrels, no drunks—just the spontaneous, unassuming joy of living in what may be the biggest temple of nature: the primeval forest of Africa. And so they have danced for thousands of years; new drums play the same old tunes, younger voices sing the same old songs.

Enough for tonight; I am going to let the melodies of the forest rock me to sleep and I will exchange my thoughts for dreams.

I am writing this as a postscript to yesterday's letter. I have had an eventful day and have at last succeeded in shooting the elephant that the pygmies so much have been longing for.

I still had the rhythm of the drums in my head when I was woken up by the old man who usually carries my gun. There must be something special about this task, as he is the only one who dares to enter my little tent.

"Fresh spoor from big elephant outside camp," he said, and pointed. I gave him the big gun, put some cartridges in my pocket, and off we went. The Wambuti himself carried a small throwing spear.

Quite right, a lone bull had passed there. The track wasn't particularly impressive, but the elephants here in the forest are not as big as those you find on the plains, and anyway it does not always follow that big tuskers have big feet, or vice versa.

We started tracking by ourselves. The first droppings we came across were warm inside, but soon we found some that were still smoking and a bit later we could hear him bringing down a tree in front of us, so he was still feeding. My little friend was now fully alerted. He advanced like a bird dog, stiff, lifting his legs high, no unnecessary movements, and I tried to imitate him as best I could.

First I saw a tail move amongst the foliage. The elephant was standing in there munching the branches from the tree he had just pushed over.

The undergrowth was very thick and it took quite some time before I, from my crouched position, could get a glimpse of his tusks. They were miserable, no more than twenty lbs. I made a sign to my companion and we withdrew silently out of earshot. I parked myself on a tree stump and said, "You saw his tusks. The government will not let me shoot such an animal. However, you have permission to kill him with your spear, and in that case I can assist you with my rifle." This was a plan the pygmy immediately agreed to. His ugly face became even uglier when his enormous grin split it into thousands of wrinkles.

Again we became bird dogs. The small spear blade was as sharp as a razor. The arm of the Wambuti was as hard as steel. The muscles stood out hard and sinewy on his small arms and his rib cage arched, broad and muscular. I had seen him before in the trees swinging from branch to branch as fast as I could move on the ground.

Normally the Wambutis don't kill elephants with a throwing spear, using instead a stabbing spear, of which there are two types, a heavier, broad-bladed one which is aimed at the heart of the animal, and a lighter one with a blade shaped like a snake's head for severing the Achilles tendon.

I had never seen a Wambuti kill, and I was now just as eager as my friend. If only the elephant would remain by his breakfast table and the freakish forest breeze stay on course! We had arrived at about seventy feet from him when he appeared to have had enough for the time being and slowly continued on his way, still chewing on his twig. We followed, close on his heels. His munching was pretty noisy, loud rumbling sounds coming from his belly, and there were cracking reports whenever he smacked his sides with his ears to chase away the clouds of insects. Then he stopped by a small tree. He caught hold of a branch as far up as he could reach, sampled it, found it satisfactory, bracketed the tree trunk with his tusks, straightened his hindlegs, and pushed the tree over, root and all, with his forehead.

This was our opportunity; the elephant was too occupied to listen carefully. He was now standing on our side of the fallen tree, broadside-on.

The Wambuti was the first to sneak forward. His bicep stood out like a tennis ball on his short upper arm when he bunched his small fist around the spear shaft. I followed immediately behind him. Never before had I been so close to an unwounded elephant. I kept the rifle at the ready, keeping my eyes fixed on the exact spot where I intended to put the bullet. As soon as the spear had left his hand, I would fire. I observed how the pygmy bent backwards, the left arm coming forward as a counterbalance. The spear whirred away, and at the same moment it entered the gray colossus he swung his trunk up and his head back towards us, but before the movement was completed the small nickel-plated bullet found its target and he fell down with a broken neck.

To my dying days I'll remember those few moments. The little man, however, showed no surprise, joy, or ecstasy—just a dignified pride. I doubt if he had even heard the shot, maybe he had forgotten it. Unfortunately, the animal fell on the spear, so I never got to know how far it had penetrated.

The Wambuti cut off the tail with his short knife, and with an august expression on his face he met the villagers who now came running. He performed a pantomime describing the sequence of events; how he had thrown his spear, how the elephant had been hit in the heart, throwing up his trunk, how I had fired as he turned towards us.

This was the small hunter's day—the day of the whole village for that matter—no neighbors would be informed. This meat, given by God and killed by themselves, was not going to be shared with any outsiders. It was going to be salted and smoked, and salt they were going to get from me. Vultures are pretty voracious, but nothing could match the gluttony with which these forty pygmies, men and women, attacked this mountain of meat with their knives and spear blades.

By evening most of the preparations for the curing of the meat had been completed. Long stands about three feet high and fashioned out of rough timber had been constructed. On these the meat, cut up in fist-sized pieces, was put. Under the shelves low burning fires were lit and maintained by the addition of green wood. In two days' time all the meat would be thoroughly cured and ready to be hid away where rain and thieving hyenas could not get at it, in hollow trees and crevices known only to the pygmies themselves.

I am more popular now; I helped the one who killed, I didn't run away, and I brought luck. Now we will get more elephants, they say, with tusks as long as palm trees and as thick as thighs.

You can have no idea with what pomp and ceremony the celebrations in honor of the little hero were held on the second day, after the meat was all prepared and ready to be eaten. Honey beer had been brewed, quantities of dry firewood had been stacked all over the place, extra drums had been borrowed from the neighboring village, and a big circle had been cleared, mowed, and swept—in other words the dance floor had been ground and polished. As you know, I am not sufficiently educated to write music, but last night I really wished I had been. There was a peculiar and almost grotesque atmosphere of excitement about this both jolly and solemn dance feast, and the feeling of the primitive and original was strengthened by the knowledge that here, so far, no white "colonial" had set foot, no tourist had gaped, and no film cameras and flashlights had disturbed the peace of this little settlement.

Here in the forest you only see the sun between eleven A.M. and two P.M. Before and after these times there is shade and half-light. A small lad climbed a liana and reached the top of a tall mahogany tree to see if the sky was clear or if rain could be expected. He came down with the news that in the east the sky was leaden and there was a lot of lightning.

Now all the men were congregating—all those over fifteen years of age. Fastened to a strip of hide fashioned from the skin of a "bush baby," they were all carrying a whistle made from a special bush. They say that the sound from these never fails to keep the rain away, and for at least five minutes there was an infernal whistling concert in all directions. Finally, however, they seemed to be convinced that the Rain God would leave them in peace.

In front of each hut everyone was engaged in the same beauty treatment. Oil and red ochre were mixed and small black bodies were anointed and changed color. The shadows became denser—perhaps the rainclouds are coming, I thought—but the pygmies didn't seem to be in the least apprehensive. More wood was put on the fires, a few handbeats on a drum, and the children came jumping forward with the same movements as their elders, happy but dignified, certainly not jolly—this was a significant and momentous day.

Finally came our hero, the elephant slayer, anointed red and shining. The drums were now in full and rhythmic beat. He came tripping along in a form of dance, every now and then skipping and jumping out to the sides. Then he paraded a couple of times around the ring on his own, whereupon the whole village with the chief in the lead arrived anointed, painted, singing, and dancing to mystical, primitive, primeval forest-music, making a ring around the hero, who now stood motionless in the center holding his spear in one hand and the tail of the elephant in the other. The dance now took the shape of a pantomime. His heroic deeds were sung in many verses—incomprehensible to me, but I got a vivid impression of what it was all about—spears were shaken, elephants fell down, meat was cut up, and the halls of the forest reverberated with music.

Only when the celebration had reached its height, when all the bodies were gleaming with sweat and shivering with excitement, did the highlight of the evening come. The beauty queen of the village, a twelve-year-old girl with budding young breasts and tremulous loins, stepped out and danced forward to meet the hero. Now everybody was in a frenzy and lost in an abandon of which only unspoilt children of nature are fully capable. I can still hear deep bass voices mingling with those more high-pitched in rapture and joy; I can still see the flames from the campfires against the dark shadows where every leaf seems to tremble in time with the rhythmic music from the drums; I can still feel the ground shaking under the tread, in perfect time, of so many small feet. What an indescribable, wild, atavistic, festive atmosphere!

At midnight there was a blinding flash of lightning, then a thunderclap as if a mountain of sheet metal had suddenly collapsed. The dancing ceased and the whistling took over—from all the whistles in the village. Abedi appeared to inspect the tent, and to be on the safe side he drove in the pegs another inch. He laughed contemptuously, as if any whistling could help, and I suspect I also smiled. But the fact remains, the thunder became more and more distant, and the small people were allowed to finish their celebrations undisturbed, until the gray dawn stole in among the trunks of the forest.

You would have enjoyed this night, my friend, as you would have understood the mood and appreciated the charm.

Yours ever,
Blix

• •

Wamba

Dick, my friend,

It is now a long time since I wrote you. I see from my diary that this was when tiny pygmies danced around a bonfire deep inside the rain forest. Much has happened since then. To start with, luck was on my side. I got big tusks and had no difficulty in recruiting porters. I had a chimpanzee as company, and Juma and Abedi had bought fifteen parrots each. They were able to get them cheaply—fifteen francs a head—and in Nairobi they will be able to sell them for a hundred and fifty to two hundred shillings. If they can just say *"jambo"* (Swahili for "hello") they are worth another fifty shillings. I bought one for you, or rather was given one by a Greek in Wamba, where I stayed for a few days. It can swear in all languages and say "Go to hell" as soon as you touch the door handle.

I had just got a license for five elephants when luck deserted me. We were now quite a caravan—my own equipment, Juma and Abedi with their girls and servants, some fifty porters, ivory ornaments, baggage, et cetera. Everybody was happy and satisfied, we had plenty of food, and we were welcome wherever we went, since we distributed meat for nothing. Apart from us, there were only Belgian and Greek traders hunting in the area, and they all sold their meat, so obviously we became more popular, and wherever we made a camp there was always a feeling of festivity around the fires at night, the pots simmered, and there was dancing till dawn. Beautiful girls, from the black man's point of view, were sent me from chiefs with plenty of elephants in their domains—unwilling girls, pretty in their way, but hurt because they had been sent as prisoners and still more hurt when they were sent back with a simple gift and a "no, thank you."

We were still in the Ituri Forest. The rains had now really broken in a big way, with one thunderstorm after another. The paths became slippery and the loads difficult to carry. The river overflowed and we had to use liana ropes to help us to cross them. In order to get the heavy lianas across we had to tow them with thin lines of tent ropes which we joined together, and thus the caravan was ferried across one load at a time. After that a raft had to be constructed to carry the ivory and equipment. Time-wasting work, and it was also cold in the water. It was extremely slippery everywhere, the food question was becoming acute, and we didn't seem to be getting anywhere. We still had a ten days' march to the next village. The black man is a child of a hot climate. You couldn't wish for a better companion if everything goes well, but in this tropical fairyland he is not used to adversities.

On the fourth day out Abedi reported that one of the porters was seriously ill. He was breathing laboriously and ran a temperature of 102. Obviously pneumonia, and I prescribed a rubdown with lukewarm towels, aspirin, and quinine, but he died that night. You know what happens when an African dies—a chorus of weeping, superstition, mumbo jumbo, et cetera. In the morning the grave was dug, and he was buried in a sitting position with his clothing and cooking utensils, his only earthly belongings.

Sadly, the caravan continued. The devil had joined us and had now taken the place of the Sun God. Nobody laughed anymore. After another two days the tragedy was repeated, and we still had another four days to the village. He survived that day but died the following night. Another day on short rations. I sent two runners to the village asking the headman to send us food. The following day two more men died. I decided to stay where I was with Abedi, his girl, and four men, and sent Juma and the rest on to buy food. The loyalty that everybody showed was remarkable; nobody wanted to leave me, but we had to have food. In six or seven days, provisions could reach us, as well as additional porters from the village.

That evening I felt poorly myself. I had been out with Abedi to try and shoot something for the pot but hadn't seen anything and returned empty-handed. I told him to make up my bed and make a fire. I was cold and shivery and knew what was in store for me—fever and bed. I could see the dead men in front of me, sitting up in their graves, before the soil was shoveled in. When my bed was made I could hardly crawl to it. "Prepare a bath for me, Abedi," I said, "close to the fire and not too hot."

When the bath was ready I took my temperature—102. I already felt confused. Again I saw the dead men, I heard weeping, and memories from my childhood came rushing back. Abedi helped me into the bath; my temperature had to be brought down. I took some aspirin and quinine and lost consciousness.

I woke up in bed when Abedi tried to make me swallow a gulp of whisky. That swig is probably what saved my life. God, how weak I was and how difficult it was to breathe. My back ached, as did both lungs. It was a bit easier when sitting up, so all we had in the way of cushions and blankets were put behind my back to prop me up. Abedi's girl was touching. She sat up all night, holding my hand, her black eyes wet with tears. I suppose she was thinking of the hour when she would help shuffle earth over me as I sat in the wet clay. How long a period passed with me semiconscious, in the grip of the fever, I don't know, but I have a feeling that it was on the fifth day that I began to think the crisis was over. I was, of course, a wreck—emaciated, hungry, and weak—but I knew Death had lost this time; I could no longer see the open grave. When I finally regained full consciousness, Suleima (the girl) was still holding my hand, and when I calmly said, "Sasa mzuri" ("Now I'm well"), and asked her to remove a few cushions so that I could stretch out properly, an angelic smile appeared on her face.

Why is it that whenever we are in great need a woman is so much more useful? Why do we get so much more comfort from her when death is near? How can she know just what to administer and how to spread comfort?

When I woke again after twenty-four hours' steady sleep, Juma had returned with the men and another ten extra men from the village. They had brought with them bananas, rice, chickens, and tomatoes in hand-woven baskets. A small girl sat in the tent opening strumming on a musical instrument, from afar you could hear the roar from the swollen river, and Juma and Abedi's parrots were having a melodious whistling match. These were my first impressions on my return to life. I was extremely weak and Suleima had to help me with everything. I could only drink tea and the odd swallow of whisky. Abedi was making buns and boiling eggs.

And so days and nights went by, and whenever required men went to the village to fetch more food for us all. Juma came in with news of elephant—phantoms carrying colossal tusks—and also spoke about big open plains which were supposed to carry big herds of the great beasts.

However, I couldn't stand on my legs and had to regain my strength first, so Suleima would have to hold my hand for a bit longer and the girl with the instrument to play back the health to mind and body.

I sent Juma out again to investigate if all he had heard really was true. He was away for a fortnight and when he came back I was sitting up in an improvised chair, made out of branches and cane; Suleima was at my side and at my feet Bao was strumming on her lute. You know Juma, you know how ugly he can get when he laughs, but what infinite goodness cannot this ugly face radiate!

"Now you're sitting up, *Bwana,*" he said when he saw me. "In a week's time you'll be shooting elephants again, because the plains are there and the bulls have tusks as thick as my thigh at the hip and as long as the biggest you shot at Masindi!"

This was good medicine. I ate chickens and eggs and drank broth and on the eighth day felt strong enough to make a move. Eight men took turns carrying me in a chair, and for short spells I walked on my own feet. Admittedly the three days' walk took us double that time, but finally we arrived at the village where they expected us. A large hut had been swept out and prepared for me and it had been stocked with chickens, bananas, rice, mangoes, and other delicacies. It was obvious that Juma had told many stories about the white man who never missed a shot and who gave away the meat.

I was completely exhausted when I went to bed that night, in a real hut with real walls and a grass roof—a palace! The fever had left me, but in its place my temperature was subnormal and I had very little strength. But I was very happy when I fell asleep that night to the tune of Bao's lute and with Suleima's long fingers in my hand.

One day at eleven A.M. Juma arrived in camp sweaty and tired but looking as if he were bringing good news, as he appeared pretty self-conscious. He squatted by my chair, spat out a long squirt of tobacco juice, and said, apropos of nothing, "The big one is standing over there not more than an hour's walk from here. If you're too tired to shoot, maybe you would just like to have a look at him. I've got the headman's carry chair and eight porters with me."

"Of course I can shoot, Juma! Take the Mannlicher and the double-barreled rifle, a water bottle, and lemons." This was the first time I had ever been carried out to a hunt, but nobody here thought it in the least odd; on the contrary, this is how chiefs and Belgian professional hunters go on safaris. The natives were probably surprised that I didn't always hunt in this way.

The carry chair was quite comfortable, consisting of a wide seat slung between two poles. The construction was such that two porters in front and two at the back could walk in single file. That way it was much easier to proceed along the narrow paths and it also made the ride more level. The spare porters walked behind and an exchange was made once every quarter of an hour. Just then I didn't weigh very much, and we went along at a leisurely pace. Juma had handed over the rifles to somebody else and he walked beside my chair smiling contentedly. This was his hunt; he had found the elephants, he had arranged for the chair and the porters—all that was left for me to do was to squeeze the trigger, and that only because he was not allowed to.

After half an hour we left the wider path that led from the village to the nearest camp and took off to our left following a well-trodden elephant path. We arrived at the low-lying plain dotted with odd palm and teak trees. The grass from last season's long dry spell had been burnt off long ago, and the new crop was already three feet high. In the depressions and shallow valleys were palm groves and clumps of trees. High termite hills and numerous mushroom-shaped antheaps, built by the vicious red ants, covered large areas. A kind of star grass with white seed pods gave a certain lustrous quality to the landscape, and the brick-red flowers of the Nandi flame tree made brilliant spots of color against the yellow-green background.

From my elevated position I had a good view of the surrounding country. After another half hour Juma slowed down a bit and, by laying a finger on his mouth, indicated that from now on we should be silent and proceed with greater caution. The tramping of naked feet on hard ground can be heard a long way, and elephants don't make any mistakes in interpreting this particular sound. I wanted to get out and walk myself, but Juma wouldn't allow me. He seemed to be of the opinion that my strength should be conserved, and as it was his day, he had his way.

When we got to high ground Juma pointed out some tall trees under which the elephant had been standing before he returned to the village. As this wasn't much more than an hour ago the bull couldn't be very far away. While the rest of us remained where we were, Juma took a man with him and went forward to reconnoiter. Everybody was now pretty keyed up and we talked in whispers. The wind was favorable and blew steadily from the west. With the field glasses, I could see that Juma had found the spoor and that the animal had walked upwind—then they disappeared over the ridge. After a while Juma's companion came into sight again, waving for us to follow. I climbed up into my chair again, and so we slowly went on. The man met us and reported that the bull had been down to a stream where he had had a bath, and that he now was standing in the sun on this side, sleeping.

The wind was still in our favor, and he had no egrets with him to give him warning of the approaching danger. Juma sat waiting two hundred yards from him. We were all absolutely silent. I was put down, took the Mannlicher myself and gave the Holland and Holland to Juma, and then we two alone approached the elephant. His tusks were not quite what I had expected from the description given to me, but they would probably weigh out at over eighty lbs., which was satisfactory. In any case there would be masses of meat for all those who so patiently had been waiting for my recovery and had so willingly helped me.

A termite hill at about fifty yards' distance from the bull became our objective. The bull was half asleep. Now and then he nodded off like an old man, but then shook himself awake again.

Walking was not at all as strenuous as I thought it would be, and the small Mannlicher felt so light that I soon changed it for the double-barreled gun, which didn't feel all that heavy either. We sat down by the termite hill. The elephant had now turned and was standing with his backside towards us. Instead of walking out to a flank, I decided to remain where I was and wait for the moment when he would present a target for a shot broadside-on. We sat there for about ten minutes in tense expectation, then he woke up and started to walk diagonally towards us. The shot was aimed at the point of the right shoulder but failed to break it, and he came charging at us in full rage. The second barrel between the eyes! He went down on his knees but got up again at the same moment I finished reloading. He stood perfectly still, as if petrified; his enormous ears were fully stretched out ready to receive the faintest sound and the pliant trunk was raised, probing in the wind. Juma and I stood motionless. Then he raised his trunk still higher, thereby exposing his chest. The bullet hit him just where the windpipe enters the chest cavity. Heart shot. He turned sideways and the next shot got him in the shoulder. He staggered away from us, and just as I was going to aim for his spine, he fell with a trumpet call which seemed a curious mixture of anger and sorrow.

Juma was pride personified. All the porters congregated, everybody shook hands, and there was much talking and chattering. Now the bad luck was broken, now we were going to get elephants. Now *Wahoga* was well again and all the elephants were out of the forest, eating grass and basking in the sun on the plains!

In the village the shots and the trumpeting of the elephant had been heard—was he dead? Yes, of course, here came Juma with the tail! The chief himself met us on our way back, and little Bao came dancing along like a sylph. She was now seven years old and badly wanted some clothes; and she'll get them after all the musical entertainment she has provided.

This evening we have all been sitting down to a conference, the outcome of which is that I am going to remain here for another few days to regain my strength and put on a bit of weight whilst Juma with a few guides goes out to reconnoiter the country and look for big tuskers.

As always,
Blix

. . . .

Dear Dick,

Last time I wrote, I believe I was pretty weak. I was transported on elephant hunts in a carry chair and could then only handle a rifle with the utmost effort.

Now I am well and strong again and can walk my black friends off their feet. It seems to me that the sun shines brighter, that the bird's song is more melodious, that the blood pulsates warmer and quicker through my veins. Sorrows and worries no longer seem insurmountable.

Juma is in splendid humor. We have shot five very good elephants, and for our simple household this means a lot. He can now, without any worries, conduct his own private pieces of business with the locals. Admittedly they get all their meat for nothing, but he can always see to it that certain advantages come his way in the form of snuff, tobacco, dark beer brewed in millet and malted with bark, nourishing and strengthening, and I can hear him whispering to some dark-skinned potentate who has just let baskets full of dried meat be carried home on the backs of members of his harem, "Beautiful girls are my weakness."

We are short of nothing in our camp. Slender girls with swinging hips carry on their heads Egyptian-formed earthenware pots filled with beer, and gifts of bananas, chickens, eggs, rice, and cooking oil are offered to us. Peace and joy are all around us. The young dance and sing, and the drums are busy. All this while the old men and myself sit in easychairs and discuss the problems of life. We talk about days gone by; so much has changed during the last fifty years, and so-called civilization, for what it's worth, has suddenly taken over most things left from tradition.

When the white man has gained the confidence of the elders and they trustfully have opened their hearts to him, then nothing can be more fascinating than to listen to their talk. They possess a primitive wisdom and natural judgment that we can never hope to learn from our books.

During a night by the campfire, when the beer has loosened the tongue, many a thought worth considering may be expressed. The blacks understand that many good things have come from us whites, but much of the new order is still foreign and difficult to comprehend. The different tribes have been forbidden to wage war against each other—the times of perpetual feuds are over. The natives can now move from area to area, from tribe to tribe, without interference; they can freely exchange their wares and carry on business. They have got medical care and hospitals, schools and roads. All this is to the good. But, they have also been introduced to a new religion, a religion which is here represented by both Catholicism and Protestantism of various sects. Little wonder that this confuses the black man. Nor is it strange why he fails to understand the white people perpetually being at war with each other and at the same time telling him that he mustn't do the same thing. Who can give him a satisfactory explanation?

It is my intention to break up here soon and move my camp to the area of Beni and Kivu, where I have obtained a license for another five elephants. I have heard so much about Kivu, and I am longing to get there. As you know, this is the only known region in Africa where the volcanoes are still active. Lake Kivu, which has given its name to the area, is supposed to be unbelievably beautiful. It is practically bottomless, with sweet crystal-clear water and completely free from the common curse of most tropical waters—the crocodile. It is situated at an altitude of 6,000 feet above sea level and the climate is the best imaginable. So far, thank God, the tourist has not discovered it, and I would like to see it in its undisturbed glory, before railways and air routes have arrived, before luxury hotels and nightclubs have grown up like poisonous fungi—before it's been tarnished and made ugly by a civilization which is unable to let things well enough alone.

Yours ever,
Blix

CHAPTER

....

8

....

Beni

My darling Cockie,

Where the road emerged into open country from the rain forest there were a small number of brick huts with thatched roofs. This is where the government officials used to live. An imposing church surrounded by smaller buildings showed that the white man's religion had come here to stay. The village street was edged by low shops, and wares of all kinds were displayed on shaded verandas. On the outskirts of the village was a small hotel and this is where we took up residence. The time was now five o'clock.

The landlord was an Italian, and over a glass of vermouth we arranged for one of the six guest huts to be put at my disposal. The main building of the hotel was only composed of dining room, lounge, bar, and office. Behind my cottage I could park my car and use an area as a camping ground for my entourage. My little cottage was quite delightful and built of burnt brick. It consisted of a big pleasant bedroom, with a good bed and mosquito net, a bathroom with a proper tub and wc, and, outside, a water cistern heated by a wood fire for the bath water.

And so we unpacked and got ourselves properly installed. For those of us who had been living so long in the bush, it was the height of luxury to again arrive back in the lap of civilization. For young Bao everything was completely new and she pottered about curiously with great big wondrous eyes. She was certain that not even the chief in Wamba had as splendid dwellings as she could see here.

The surroundings here are beautiful, with undulating terrain. Impressive cliff formations alternate with green valleys and plains. To the north we have the dark and massive primeval forests, and to the east the great Ruwenzori complex can be seen behind more friendly ridges in their spring finery. Just now the snow-clad mountaintops are colored pink by the last rays of the descending sun.

At six o'clock people began to gather on the veranda of the hotel and the landlord introduced me to the ones he thought I ought to meet. He was particularly keen that I should get to know the Belgian chief veterinary officer of the district, who was also a great elephant hunter and knew the country between Kivu and Ruwenzori particularly well and therefore was in a position to give me many good tips.

It was nice to converse with a white man again and particularly pleasant to meet somebody who had common interests. The vet told me that now was the right time to hunt here, as in a month's time the grass would be too long, making it difficult to see the tusks. There were plenty of elephant about, he told me, but one had to be up early to see them on the plains, or alternatively, keep watch from the edge of the forest in the evenings in order to earmark the big bulls. He kindly offered to lend me two of his own local guides.

We had dinner together—fried chicken with spaghetti and new potatoes swallowed down with a bottle of Chianti. Afterwards coffee and brandy on my private little veranda. The Belgian was of the opinion that the biggest elephants were to be found inside the forest, as the big bulls seldom ventured out onto the plains, but that hunting in there was not easy. However, I knew that there were plenty of Wambuti in the vicinity, so did not think I would have any problems on that score.

When I woke up the following morning, the promised guides were already waiting, and after an early cup of tea we drove out in the truck in the direction of Kivu. Soon I left the road and went cross-country over more broken country. It was beautiful out there in the early morning with the glittering dew and long shadows. Dark clumps of trees made sharp silhouettes against the clear blue sky and between them the rolling green plains stretched out. On the slopes were a few native villages with well-tended banana groves, and from invisible huts blue smoke was rising.

About three miles from Beni there is a high isolated hill, and this we climbed. From there we got a good view of the surrounding country. We could see quite a few elephants that were still out in the open, but evidently they were on their way to a thickly foliaged valley. Their tusks showed up brilliantly in the sunshine, but none of them were of tempting size.

After about an hour we returned to the road, which we followed in order to get to know the terrain. Soon we were in broken, mountainous

From left to right: Bror, the Prince of
Wales, and Denys Finch Hatton.
The white disk on the front of the
train was to reflect the sun and to
keep the passengers cool. (*Jacqueline
Hoogterp*)

"I have had so many tame
chimpanzees . . ." (*Jacqueline Hoogterp*)

Freddie Guest was very enamored of airplanes, and had two Gypsy Moths brought out from England for the safari. *(Jacqueline Hoogterp)*

The Prince of Wales's safari, 1928.
(Jacqueline Hoogterp)

Denys Finch Hatton (center) with
the Prince of Wales and his aide-de-
camp. *(Jacqueline Hoogterp)*

Cockie. *(Jacqueline Hoogterp)*

Bror and Cockie at their cottage at
Babarti.

Kuhnert's *Elephant*

country, and here we found elephant tracks and droppings almost everywhere.

By ten o'clock I was back again and had a good breakfast on my veranda. I told the guides to look for elephants in the area we had just visited and to report back immediately if they saw anything with good tusks. In order to give them an indication of what I required, I showed them the ivory I had with me.

Later, I took with me Juma, Marube, and young Bao, who spoke the Wambuti language fluently, on a trip along the road and into the forest. At the first village we reached there were no Wambutis, but a reliable-looking man told me that there were plenty of elephants in the vicinity and only two nights ago they had raided the banana groves. The tracks were still there, and to make sure that he spoke the truth, we followed him to the place. Quite right, two bulls had been there and caused quite a lot of damage. This was thick forest, and the ground was fairly hilly.

In the village Bao had purchased a basket full of eggs and a big bunch of bananas, and when we came back two small boys were chasing a cockerel, for which Bao had just offered three francs. When the bargaining and chase had been concluded we continued on to the next village, a further five miles on our way.

It really was amazingly beautiful in there in the forest with all its abundant vegetation. Slender oil palms, straight imposing mahogany trees between which the lianas hung in immense nets, majestic teaks with their rough dark-brown bark and softly rounded crowns from which the branches slope downwards—hence the native name of M'vuli (umbrellas).

In the next village there were Wambutis and, while Bao walked about and talked to the pygmies, we discussed the hunting possibilities with the chief. Marube tempted him with promises of free meat and Juma showed him with signs the length of tusk we required. It takes a little time to converse with these primitive souls, as they have never been used to hurrying over anything in their somewhat monotonous lives. However, there seemed to be plenty of elephant about, and the pygmies said they knew where they could be found in the daytime after their nightly raids in the banana groves. We finally came to the conclusion with the chief that he should send in reports every morning if any big elephant had been spotted. Then we visited another two villages, where the same arrangement was made. With the help of our two borrowed guides we had now put out feelers covering a fairly substantial area.

At dawn every day I sent out Marube and the driver to gather the information of what had happened during the night in the different villages, and by ten o'clock I had the collated reports. Then the day was passed investigating this intelligence. The first day I followed the pygmies deep into the forest and observed several bulls, but none of them proved to be big enough. In the meantime Juma was out on the plains with my best pair of field glasses, but he also failed to see anything worth shooting.

In this way we hunted for a week and the result was two good pairs of tusks. It was all hard work and we had to make long tiring walks over difficult country and through muddy swamps and almost impenetrable palm vegetation.

One day I came across a glorious sight. On a fallen tree trunk, right out in the middle of a swamp, a leopard was lying sunning himself. His hide shone like gold in the bright sunshine, which was filtered through the foliage of the treetops high above. A small stream bubbled under the tree and the wavelets gleamed like silver. The ripple of the water had deadened the sound of our approach and the leopard was ignorant of our presence. The gentle breeze which reached us was also moving the palm fronds, which made sounds like distant zither music. Marube handed me the small Mannlicher, and so with a single shot I ruined this charming scene.

I now had four good skins and, with an additional two, they would make a nice rug or a beautiful fur coat.

The Wambutis told us that about two days' march to the south there was a mountain which they called Okiti, and here there were lots of elephants. Before this, every time we had tracked an animal for a long time without making contact they whispered to each other that surely he had gone off to Okiti.

I therefore thought it might be a good idea to recruit some porters and go there and stay for a week or so. Maybe the pygmies would be right, because elephants like high country, and in any case such a safari would break the monotony of the present routine. One evening I spoke to a government official and he promised to get me twenty-five porters. I bought rice and maize flour in the shop and Abedi and the girls who were in charge of the housekeeping were made busy purchasing other necessities. Eggs and a lot of clucking hens had already been procured. I also selected four of the Wambuti hunters whom I had found most useful during the last week. After two days of preparations we were ready and left Beni on foot.

Whenever I walk through the rain forest I come under the spell of its mysterious beauty. White lilies brighten the valleys and thousands of multicolored orchids flower in the clefts of trees. Enormous ferns shoot up between moss-covered boulders and lichen hangs down like great beards from tree trunks and branches. In hundreds of streams the water bubbles crystal clear, the birds sing, and the parrots whistle in tune.

Somebody has said that Africa is the continent where the birds don't sing, the flowers have no scent, and the women no beauty. I can only declare that whoever has expressed this opinion has never walked through fragrant fields of lilies, never listened to the beautiful flutelike song of the white-browed robin chat, and has never seen a woman from Somalia or Marua.

The Marua tribe comes to my mind as my landlord of the hotel had a so-called *menagere* from Marua and she was certainly beautiful. A *menagere* is apparently somebody who is included in every white bachelor's establishment in the Congo and her duties are identical to those of a wife except for the involvement of the clergy. She keeps all keys to stores, larders, and cupboards, and generally supervises the management of the house— and at night she sleeps in the master's bed.

Nearly all the women from the Marua district are good-looking. Their features are not as finely chiseled as the Somali or other Hamitic tribes, but their faces are pretty and their bodies softly rounded and well-formed. They are well aware of the fact that they are the beauties of the Congo.

Abedi, however, maintains that the girls from Wamba are best. They cook the best food, and in addition they have oblong skulls bent slightly backwards, which he says is a great advantage as they can sleep on one's shoulder without causing cramp.

At midday we rested by a wide stream, but the water was shallow enough for us to wade across. There were plenty of elephant tracks there and we also saw spoor from okapi and giant forest hog. The trees were teeming with monkeys and they followed us with great interest, swarming along the branches easily, swinging from the lianas, and making tremendous jumps from tree to tree, all the time gibbering and chattering away. I feel sure they must have been wondering what our safari was doing in the middle of the rain forest where there were no roads and no well-defined paths.

Young Bao was well pleased, because in her opinion monkey meat was the best of all food. Fried "a la Wamba"—roasted whole over hot embers with hair, hide, and entrails remaining intact and then hung for two days. Okay by me as long as the carcass wasn't hanging too close to my sleeping quarters.

At four o'clock we stopped for the day. At that time dusk was already beginning to set in in the forest, where the massive treetops create an impenetrable screen against the sinking sun. The porters' loads were put down in long rows, *pangas** (rather like the Indian *kukri*), and axes were taken out and a clearing was made for the camp. The siting of a forest camp must be made with a certain amount of circumspection. One should avoid the vicinity of trees with heavy dried-out branches which may fall down, and there is also a certain variety of creeper that crawls up the trunks and, after reaching the top, produces a fruit, in size and weight rather like a coconut. Not very pleasant to be hit on the head with one of these. No tents are required here. The forest provides everything needed for the putting up of a shelter or hut. The big parchment-like leaves from the phrynia plant serve as the ideal roofing material, lianas and fibrous plants are used as ropes and binding material, and young saplings as up-rights and roofing supports.

In the kitchen department a couple of big fires were lit, which later died down to glowing embers and from which occasional flames made the overhanging foliage vibrate with heat. Water was fetched from a stream nearby, and the Wambutis went out in search of honey. Soon a small collection of huts had grown up and when darkness fell the camp was lit up by a dozen fires. Ghostly shadows danced between the dark trees; the smoke was sucked upwards to be taken away by the gentle night breeze above the treetops.

All had had light loads to carry and nobody was tired, not even young Bao, who already was twanging on her lute, accompanied by a small Wambuti who was sitting by her side playing mournful tunes on his bam-boo flute. Chicken curry with rice for supper, followed by coffee and a whisky, and then undisturbed sleep on a bed of soft moss.

In the forest the dew falls early and heavily, and in the morning more dry wood was added to the fading campfires, which soon took new life and flamed up again. The blankets were dried out, Abedi served a warm-ing cup of early morning tea, and breakfast was prepared. There was no hurry. Everybody knew his own job; there was no need for orders to be

---

Panga: a long, curved knife.

given or for unnecessary shouting. The half-wild people of the forest work silently and efficiently and conversations are carried out in whispers.

At eight o'clock the safari was on the move, and we followed a small river running in a southwesterly direction. We came across more and more elephant tracks, and soon came into a big open wood with very little undergrowth. The trees were very like our chestnuts. This was camphor wood and from the bark the pygmies distill a red dye which they sell, at great profit, to all the tribes, who use it for ceremonial purposes at organized dances and for war paint. It was also ideal country for elephant hunting, as you had good vision for twenty to thirty yards in all directions.

Still following the stream's windings, we arrived at noon at a bigger river. Here we halted, and while Abedi was preparing lunch, Juma, myself, and two Wambutis went out on a reconnaissance. We out here are as ignorant of the way the elephant is going to take, as we at home are of the direction the hare is going to follow.

The elephant tracks were now becoming more numerous and at a small swamp we came upon a very big bull spoor from the previous day. A little further on we also found fairly fresh buffalo tracks.

Suddenly, I saw the small Wambuti walking in front freeze with one foot poised in the air. Automatically we all stopped and followed the direction of his gaze. About twenty yards further on I got a glimpse of something yellow between the leaves, lit up by a ray of sunshine in the twilight. What could it be? Then something moved and I could discern the ear of a red buffalo. Slowly Juma placed the Mannlicher in my hands. Should I fire? A shot would frighten the elephants away. On the other hand it would mean beautiful buffalo steaks, and the porters would be so pleased to get meat. Juma softly whispered in my ear, "The elephants have never heard a shot fired and do not know the consequences." Perhaps. Still, I could only see the ear and get a glimpse of some yellow between the leaves. The Wambuti in front had let his foot sink to the ground, and now he slowly lifted an arm, pointing to his right. There, we now saw, stood another buffalo staring at us, and with his head out in the open, completely free from the surrounding vegetation. I could see how his nose was twitching as he tried to get our wind. Then he pawed the ground as a warning to the others, which had immediate effect. Stirring noises came from the undergrowth and we could see the branches swaying. The bull himself, however, remained standing as I raised the Mannlicher. I aimed at a point immediately below his chin and the solid bullet penetrated and broke his neck. He collapsed as if hit by lightning, and the others immediately and noisily disappeared.

I went up to my quarry. This was a red dwarf buffalo, which carries a beautifully proportioned head with horns flattened at the base and long smooth tips directed upwards. He is supposed to be more aggressive than any other variety of his species, but so far I have not been attacked by a single one in spite of the fact that I have shot quite a few for meat during my wanderings in the rain forest when after elephant and okapi. This, however, may be just by pure chance. The big black buffalo of East Africa, on the other hand, has often showed an inclination to aggressiveness, particularly on occasions when it was least welcome.

We now went back to the rest of the safari and I gave orders for camp to be made. We chose a lovely place with a splendid view of the river, which there was about a hundred yards wide and fell over cliffs into shallow waters. I sent Marube with ten men to the dead buffalo to collect the meat and the hide. The latter would be used for making straps, which on a foot safari always come in handy for fastening loads, et cetera. When dried, salted, stretched, and oiled with fat they become very pliable and hard-wearing.

I continued my reconnoitering during the afternoon. The numerous tracks showed that there were plenty of elephant about and they seemed to be concentrated around the swamp and the wide slopes above. The ground there is waterlogged and probably slightly salty, and salt attracts all game. By a typical and obviously well-frequented salt lick I also found spoor from bongo, the most attractive animal in the rain forest, and from the giant forest hog.

By the time I returned the camp was ready, and buffalo meat was being roasted on grates made out of hardwood over low-burning charcoal. Particularly succulent pieces had been pierced by sharpened saplings which had been stuck in the ground close to the fire. In my own kitchen the pots and pans were gently bubbling on some stones placed over the glowing embers and the girls were busy peeling potatoes nearby.

We were in elephant country, and as little noise as possible was the order of the day. One spoke seldom and then only in whispers. The campfires were kept low. Just very scanty shelters had been put up as protection from the heavy morning dew.

My bed of moss had been prepared under a roof of grass and leaves and the mosquito net rigged up on four sticks. Outside the perimeter of light cast by the campfires stood the forest dark and silent, but there were a few stars twinkling kindly through a gap in the dense foliage overhead. Soon everything was quiet and one could only hear the munching from black faces, a sound that gradually turned into gentle snoring. The rifles, cleaned and oiled, had been placed by my bedside, and with sleepy eyes I could observe the embers under Abedi's pots slowly die down.

There was something very restful about my small camp, giving me a feeling of happiness to be alive. Half awake, I heard the sounds of different animals moving in the dark and, to the chirps of the cicadas, I finally went to sleep.

I woke up from a warning shout. Within a few seconds the entire camp was aroused and dry twigs were thrown on the still smoldering embers. "*Siafu* [the soldier or safari ant]—the *siafu* is here!" There was a long train of this most dreaded of insects—the real master of the African jungle—outside. I fumbled after my electric torch. The outside of the mosquito net was black with ants, but so far none had gotten inside. All around the camp the natives were running and jumping about stark naked, driven to a frenzy by the bites from these terrible creatures. Quickly, all available receptacles were filled with hot ashes from the fires, and these in turn were strewn in a magic circle all around the camp. Fire and hot ashes are the only things that will halt the advance of these dreadful marauders. The Wambutis hurriedly made torches from twisted grass and dry sticks, and these were lit and put across the ants' line of advance.

In the meantime Abedi and the girls tried to salvage everything that was eatable. At last fire and the hot ashes stopped any further advance, but the cut-off forces within the perimeter did not surrender. Inside the circle they were everywhere—on the ground, in the beds, even on the long sloping branches of the trees. All these would have to be liquidated. More fire, more hot ashes, would have to be put down. So far I was safe under my net, but it was only a question of time before they found a way through the leaves and got in amongst the blankets. They are very difficult to kill, since they will let themselves be pulled apart rather than relax their grip on living flesh. It was a hellish night and there was no possibility of sleep. When at last dawn had come there were still thousands of ants crawling about.

The *siafu* or safari ants are the most terrible creatures, with jaws like pincers, and are a menace to man and animal alike all over East and Central Africa. You find them in wooded areas, where they live in holes underground. At certain times of the year they go off on long marches in which the entire colony participates. In the lead are the combat forces, followed by the workers carrying eggs and well protected on either flank by soldiers specially detailed for this purpose.

These creatures are born without fear. They are so numerous that perhaps our Lord thought it unnecessary to provide them with this quality. They attack everything alive, even pachyderms. The elephant hates and detests them, as they attack all the soft places where he cannot get at them. They crawl up the trunk, earholes, and eye sockets and cause excruciating pain. The safari ants are particularly on the move during the rainy season, and at the beginning of this period it can be sheer hell to walk through the forest. Possibly their migrations at these times are due to the fact that their underground dwellings get filled with water and they have to look for other places to live. When they reach a watercourse they follow this till they come to a place where a fallen tree or something similar provides a means of crossing. When the *siafu* is on the move the elephant and rhino leave the forest for more open country in order to get away from these little red devils. Nothing stops them—except fire and hot ashes. A stabled animal has absolutely no chance against them, and they can finish off a horse, leaving just the skeleton, in a matter of hours.

The rain forests of the Congo teem with ants of all kinds, colors, and sizes, and they are permanently at war with each other. Such fratricidal combats generally finish with one side being completely exterminated. However, we humans are no better than these ants, and they—as well as we—will probably continue with our wars as long as there is life on this earth.

All living things appear to be afflicted by this same curse—mammals, fish, reptiles, birds, and humans. Even germs fight each other, but their war assists the human in finding remedies against illness and pests.

As soon as it was light we started to clean up after the ants. Everything had to be shaken out, scoured, brushed, and polished. The surrounded ants within the perimeter of ashes were still in evidence, crawling about in their thousands. Inch by inch they took over the camp and we had to evacuate and move to another site. This task was left to Abedi, whilst Juma, the pygmies, and myself went hunting.

We forded the river and headed in the direction where we had seen the animals licking salt. On the way we surprised a family of chimpanzees who were searching for insects and other goodies between stones and tree stumps. They immediately ran away, but as they are very inquisitive we got further glimpses of them when they would now and then stop behind the screen of foliage to take another peep at us. I have had so many tame chimpanzees that I feel very friendly towards them.

At about ten o'clock we came upon the fresh spoor of two bulls. The droppings were cold but nevertheless fairly recent, possibly three to four hours old. A bit further on there were a couple of uprooted trees, so they couldn't have been far away.

Two hours later we heard them—long regular reports of puffing and wheezing. The pygmy in front turned around and with a grin said, "They're asleep and snoring." There was no wind and we could walk right up to them.

They were lying in an open clearing back to back, with a small round antheap between them serving as a pillow to them both. It was a sight I'll remember for a long time. Here were these two giants, resting peacefully. Forgotten were all worries about pygmies, spears and traps, and the firearms of the white man.

I had to make a detour in order to inspect the ivory. One carried long blackened tusks, but not particularly thick; those of the other one, however, were magnificent. I would have to fire at the biggest first, but how? When he was lying down? Perhaps. I could aim for a heartshot, but how would the other one react? How could I get them both?

I didn't have to consider the alternatives for long. The big one emitted an immense snore and woke up. First he raised himself leisurely on his forelegs and then with a jerk he was up on all fours. There he stood, the giant, not much more than thirty feet away. Before a puff of wind or something else had time to ruin my chance, I fired at his shoulder. He rushed forward with a tremendous bound and disappeared in the forest. The other one woke up at the report from my rifle, and when his head showed behind the antheap he got a bullet in the brain and collapsed with a tremendous thud which made the ground shake. At the same time, from the dimness of the forest, came the sound of the first one falling and a loud trumpet call telling us that he was dead.

It had all happened so quickly, and for a long while we just stood about looking at each other. Then the spell was broken and we went up to the dead animals. The tusks of the one by the antheap were long and uniform with good ivory, but the other one lying fifty yards from the edge of the forest carried a really magnificent pair of tusks. They were almost completely straight, with a great spread between the tips, and would certainly weigh out at a hundred and thirty lbs. apiece.

One of the pygmies was sent back to the camp in advance in order to spread the good news. Soon the drums would begin to speak and there would be relays from village to village and hungry small black people would hasten to the mountains of meat.

By two o'clock I was back in camp, and as darkness falls early in the forest, I decided to stay till the following morning, when I hoped to make Beni in one day.

I sent my porters to the dead elephants so that they could get their share of the meat and an opportunity to feast all night, but warned them to be back by dawn. Marube was told to supervise the removal of the tusks and arrange for their transportation to Beni.

It would be good to sleep after the hideous night with the ants, and my bed was prepared with additional moss and grass. The flames from the fires were already licking the overhanging branches, the black girls were busy in the kitchen grilling succulent buffalo steak, and young Bao was gently strumming on her lute accompanied by the Wambuti on his flute. After an early dinner I was stretched out on my blankets having day-dreams about this lovely rain forest, silent, dark, and moist, where quiet crystal-clear streams smoothly flowed down to the Ituri River to be joined by the majestic Congo and were finally carried the long distance to the Atlantic.

The play of light and shadows along the tree trunks and branches, the different and forever changing sounds from animals at night, the varying tunes from Bao's lute merged together into a drowsy symphony until deep and restful sleep took over.

Next morning we started early. We took with us only what was necessary for our immediate use—the rest Abedi would have to take care of. One of the Wambuti guided us and just before dark we were back in Beni. Here we found a telegram from Charles Markham announcing his arrival four days hence.

I managed to get two bulls on the third day.

The first one I got in the morning when the dew still lay heavy on the grass and the sun had just risen over the horizon. He was standing at the edge of a wood, wet and black after the night's wandering in the long grass and enjoying the first warm rays of sunshine. I myself sat on a small hillock at a distance of some hundred yards, which provided rest for both elbows and rifle—a situation which we hunters dream about but seldom experience.

The other one I encountered in the afternoon in a tall fringe of woods by the riverbed. There were six animals in all, two bulls and four cows. On both sides there were deep defiles, and in a couple of places cliffs from where you could get a good view of both slopes. I sent a couple of scouts on a detour, telling them to drive the elephants towards the cliff where I had placed myself. They were experienced hunters and succeeded in making the elephants walk past me. The biggest bull was killed by two bullets and the others rushed back to the sheltering woods.

Whether it was the natives, the elephants, or the crack from the rifle that had frightened him, I do not know, but the moment the bull fell, a big leopard came bounding out of the woods and up the opposite slope. Juma handed me the Mannlicher, which I automatically brought up to the firing position. The first bullet was high, the second too far to the right. When the leopard saw the dust rising after the impact, he took a tremendous leap right into the small sand cloud and this became his undoing. The next second he rolled with a broken neck to the bottom of the valley.

It was too late in the day to have him skinned then and there, so we just tied his legs together, slid a pole through the ropes, and carried him to the truck which was waiting about a mile further on.

When we got to Beni in the evening I found Markham already there. He had arrived a day earlier than expected, and had with him mail, newspapers, and books. I had a lot to tell, and Charles wanted to know everything about my latest adventures. There was champagne with the dinner, and we invited as guests the district commissioner and my friend the veterinary elephant hunter.

The night was brilliantly clear and I thought the stars were twinkling closer than ever. In the far distance, Ruwenzori's snow-clad summit showed in the moonlight.

We stayed in Beni for another three days, during which time we shot our fifth elephant. Then we said good-bye to our friends and continued to Kivu—the ultimate aim of our safari.

All my love,
Blix

CHAPTER

9

· ·

Lake Kivu

My dear Dick,

Marube and the girls left early for Wamba. Leave-takings are never
pleasant, but in this case the sadness was somewhat relieved by the giving
of presents, cured meat, clothes, a gramophone with records . . . and
promises of an early return. Abedi and Juma packed our things and loaded
everything into the Buick while we had our breakfast on the veranda and
paid our bills.

The route to Kivu is very beautiful; magnificent scenery which is easy
to take in, as the road winds along valleys and mountain slopes. It is a rich
country to which numerous natives have moved with their families and
domestic animals in order to grow crops which find a ready market
amongst the labor forces of nearby gold mines. You see entire mountain
slopes planted with bananas, and below are big maize fields. The climate
is healthful and the rainfall is well distributed; in addition the land is
adequately watered by rivers, streams, and lesser watercourses, many of
them with waterfalls and rapids which could provide power. Here there
must be great possibilities for development if the problem of transport
could be overcome. Minority tribes which are now isolated could be
given an opportunity to expand.

Vine wrote in his book that Roosevelt's New Deal has made America
discard her child's clothing, and now it's about time that Africa as well put
on something new and more adult. Here there are two major problems to
solve: the sleeping sickness, the pest that is a menace to humans and
animals alike, and transport. The latter is of tremendous importance not
only from an economic point of view. It constitutes a significant factor in
education and modern development.

Fifty years ago Africa was a jumble of different small tribes, all speaking different languages and perpetually at war with each other. Now they can travel by road and river under peaceful conditions, trade with each other, and buy wives reciprocally; old wrongs and old hates have been forgotten and disappeared. One can but wonder why things have not developed in this way amongst us Europeans. The more two people see of each other, the more they should learn to understand each other. Their general outlook in life becomes wider and greater. The reasons for warfare must be diminished if youth is to be educated to believe that friendship and tolerance are better than implacability and hate. We have seen striking examples of this theory in Africa, not to mention the great continent of America and the British Empire.

A railway network covering Africa would cost billions; to make it possible to transport produce by rail and to organize cheap passenger fares would mean heavy state subsidies, but compared to armament costs and wars, how very cheap, particularly if in this way one could solve the problems of living space and famines and contribute to a greater understanding and tolerance among people. The day farseeing governments allow "flat rates" for the produce from Equatorial Africa on worldwide markets, then what tremendous possibilities will not open up for the Congo, French Central Africa, the still untouched areas in Kenya and Tanganyika, the Portuguese colonies in the west and east, and the rich Cameroons.

That afternoon we arrived in Kivu and got rooms in the annex of the packed hotel. The small town is not pretentious. The houses have been built in a haphazard manner without any architectural planning and the streets follow the same pattern, or rather the lack of it. The surroundings, however, are more magnificent than one could imagine in one's most fanciful dreams. They are a conglomeration of Como, Geneva, Vesuvius, Fuji, and the Alps, a panorama of infinite dimensions. This is nature showing off in all her beauty and splendor.

In the evening we strolled along the shore and went for a short drive along the eastern road, which is so narrow that a vehicle can just pass along it. And later, having a drink in the small bar, Markham, owner of coal mines in Yorkshire, speculator, and multi-millionaire, imagined a future Kivu, a Kivu that would cause people to desert the beaches of Cannes and Biarritz and the gaming tables at Monte Carlo and Palm Beach. Without a doubt Kivu is a more attractive place when compared to most other tourist resorts and would have every possibility of becoming one of the world's leading centers in this particular sphere, once speedy communications linked it to the four corners of the world.

Next morning there was a black cloud above the top of one of the craters to the east. From one of the nearest hills one could observe that the bottom of the cloud was glowing. Soon the natives arrived with news. A thick stream of lava was overflowing from the rim of the crater and was on its way down towards the lake. This was a phenomenon that had not occurred for many years. Last time there had been an eruption it had risen to such a temperature that most living things had perished.

A while later it was reputed that still another stream of lava had erupted on the other side of the crater and was now working its way in a wide sweep down towards the lake.

That afternoon a plane arrived with newspaper reporters from Nairobi. As I knew the pilot, I arranged for a trip over the mountain. It was an unforgettable experience. Like two enormous glowing rivers of molten steel from a giant blast furnace, the two streams of lava slowly flowed down the mountainside and out over the low-lying country. Fallen trees were burning, clouds of smoke from steam and gases were hanging over the glowing mass, and from the inside of the mountain rose a thick cloud of ashes which was quickly dispersed by the northeasterly wind.

Next day we left for Nairobi, past Lake Edward, through the districts of Uganda, over Jinja and the Ripon Falls, where the Nile starts the long journey to the Mediterranean, along the northern shores of Lake Victoria, and so into Kenya and over the highlands down to Nairobi.

Twice we had difficulties with locust swarms. Although we had a saloon car, so the windows could be pulled up, the insects were sucked in through the radiator grill and caused the engine to stall. They were big and yellow and by then had finished off all the crops and vegetable matter they had found on their way. They arrived like a devastating tempest. If you are at some distance from the swarm, the sun will illuminate the body colors of the insects, making them glitter and shine. Should you, however, happen to get into a large swarm (the biggest I have experienced was sixty miles long with a frontage of ten miles) the sun gets completely obscured and everything becomes gray and dark. For ten long miles we worked our way through this scourge of God and one thought of the punishment of Egypt and St. John in the desert. What a meal this would have been.

The natives devour locust like we eat prawns, but raw. Not having tried them I don't know what they taste like. But what a pest! One knows how quickly the ordinary caterpillar can defoliate our gardens. Imagine a three-inch-long flying machine with jaws strong enough to bite through the thickest stalk. Everything in their way is devastated, and they ravage from the Cape in the south to the northernmost part of Africa. In gigantic clouds you see them flying over, pursued by countless birds of prey— eagles, hawks, vultures, kites, buzzards, and also by big flocks of our Nordic storks. I once caught a stork from such a flock on the Serengeti. I suppose it had got hurt in some way, or otherwise just overeaten. It had a ring round one leg, showing it had been marked in Denmark.

The locust constitutes a serious menace to agriculture and is one of the great problems in rich Equatorial Africa. There exists a Pan-African organization for the combating of this scourge, and one of its chief tasks is finding the breeding grounds to which the insects retire to lay their eggs once their flying phase is finished. Deep trenches are then dug, into which the newly hatched hoppers are driven and where they then are destroyed by poison or other means. Fields over which the hoppers are estimated to advance are also sprayed from the air with arsenic. This, of course, also destroys the grazing for domestic animals as well as wildlife.

Difficulties and problems in these countries are nearly always connected with insects. Flies transmit sleeping sickness, mosquitoes malaria and yellow fever; but in Panama, where the death rate was enormous, the yellow fever has been brought under control, and in the East Indies the cotton and rubber plantations are now almost fever-free. The transmitter of the sleeping sickness, the tsetse fly, must have shade to live and the malaria mosquito's larva can only develop in stagnant water. Therefore we have two weapons in the war against these carriers of deadly diseases— drainage and clearing of the bush.

Yours ever,
Blix

CHAPTER

··

10

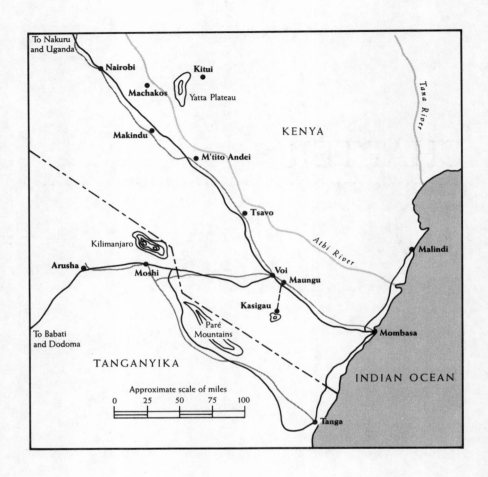

To Nakuru
and Uganda

Nairobi

Kitui

Machakos

Yatta Plateau

KENYA

Makindu

M'tito Andei

Tama River

Tsavo

Malindi

Kilimanjaro

Atbi River

Arusha

Moshi

Voi

Maungu

Kasigau

To Babati
and Dodoma

Paré
Mountains

Mombasa

TANGANYIKA

INDIAN OCEAN

Approximate scale of miles

0   25   50   75   100

Tanga

. . . .

Tsavo

My darling Cockie,

I am now staying at Tsavo, where I have not been for several years. Some time ago I was up at Kitui, situated to the northwest of this vast area of bush, discussing elephants with old Makula, Simba, and his brother Gondo, the most experienced hunters in this part of the world. They are all dedicated hunters apart from being poachers and smugglers of deadly poisons. Fine old rascals! However, they loved their hazardous profession and the excitement they got out of it. The fact that the police were always after them only made their work still more fascinating.

I had arrived from Machakos and had taken with me a Kikuyu who knew where Makula's home was, well hidden as it was amongst the thorn-bush so that no unwelcome visitor could find it. It was close to sundown and of course Makula was not at home. His two wives, one old and one young, had no idea of his whereabouts but said he would probably be back within a fortnight or a month. This was only what I had expected them to say. Old Abedi, who was with me, prepared a simple camp—a sleeping bag in the soft sand, one empty box for a table, and another for a chair. I had shot a francolin on my way there and this provided the main supper course. Abedi was given five shillings to buy a goat from my suspicious hostesses and another five for the procurement of beer and honey, if available. As elephants and bees share the same environment the native elephant hunter nearly always has honey stored away. It makes the strongest beer and can be gathered on non-hunting days.

When the francolin was ready to be served, a slender girl with a springy step and undulating hips arrived carrying a clay pitcher on her head. She could have stepped straight out of an Egyptian frieze. An old woman produced a beautifully fashioned jar full of honey and made out of bark. A boy and a small girl led a reluctant and braying goat. More wood was added to the campfire. Abedi started bargaining, maintaining that for five shillings we ought to get two pitchers of beer and twice as much honey, and as for the goat—it was not even worth slaughtering. The Swahili businessman always runs true to form. I told Abedi that we should be grateful to our hostesses for having been able to provide anything at all but that I would now engage them in conversation whilst he prepared a large pot of tea with an ample quantity of sugar as a feast for them.

The women came from the coast and as I had been to their home village we had no difficulty in getting on together. We sat and discussed the rhythmic beat of the waves against the shore, the Arab dhows, the slave markets, and the ivory which was smuggled out of the country. We talked about the beauty of the moon being reflected in the water just beyond the surf during the month before the monsoon, and about the feeling of security one experienced here in the bush where no police *askari* could find those who knew how to hide themselves and who knew the art of surviving under bush conditions. The arm of the law had as yet not reached this far. I said it was a well-known fact that their man, old Makula, was the only one who was able to find his way and to hunt here. I told them that I had heard his name mentioned far away on the other side of the ocean, where the dhows brought the ivory he had sold. We spoke of Makula's old friend Bwana Mogu, the white hunter of the same big game, and how it was he who had first told me about Makula and that this was the reason for me now being there. I explained that I also would like to send ivory across the ocean with the Arab dhows. The beer ran out, so we had to get more, lots more, as the distrustful attitude of my audience seemed to be wearing off. I was quite certain that within an hour or two Makula would have an account of our talk.

A small girl twanged a stringed instrument known along the coasts of all tropical countries. A sad tune accompanied by an equally melancholy lyric—an interpretation of the sea's cool kisses on a lonely shore. The cigarettes gleamed, the beer took effect. The women already believe Makula will not be away for all that length of time. More dry grass is added to the campfire, it becomes lighter, and the cooked bird is served. The teapot is handed around. This is the way to become friendly in the bush.

The next morning Makula was there and with him were Simba and Gondo—and so the talk of elephants began. This is how my desire to get to know the great Taru desert was born—the country between the Athi and the Tana—the rivers that run from the Kitui highlands all the way to the sea.

After that, these three and myself along with my small group of followers walked this area for a full three months. What, however, is three months if you want to explore a plain a hundred and eighty miles long by a hundred and twenty miles wide, covered in parts with almost impenetrable bush? I gradually came to realize that these three, although they had hunted here for almost thirty years and also had inherited the experiences of other hunters before them, only had a scant knowledge of the area. They could travel here when the rains had filled the waterholes, otherwise not.

When I got back to Nairobi and met Beryl Markham we decided to explore this ground together from the air. There were landing strips at Makindu, Tsavo, and Voi, all situated by the railway line and approximately fifty miles apart from each other. As the first order of business it was decided to establish these three places as bases and accordingly we dispatched by train petrol, oil, and camp equipment for us two and a mechanic. You know what these regions are like and can therefore appreciate that this was a somewhat hazardous venture. Forced landings cannot be made anywhere—the country is uninhabited and waterless apart from the Athi River—so should we be forced down the chances of survival were remote. But, as you know, Beryl is not the type to get scared easily. We intended to make money in the future from the experiences we were now about to gain—and money we both needed.

The aircraft, a two-seater open Avian, belonged to Beryl and I was to be responsible for the cost of petrol, the mechanic, and the camp. Nobody was to be informed of the results of the reconnaissance.

Our first camp was at Makindu and for more than one week we flew five hours every day, two and a half hours in the morning and the same in the afternoon. In order not to be overloaded at takeoff we only fueled for flights of approximately three hours' duration. Close to Makindu we could daily observe a herd of some twenty elephants and they soon became as familiar as domestic pets. Our own flyovers did not seem to bother them, but from time to time a few of them would shake their heads and gaze skywards as if contemplating whether this noise could possibly be thunder. However, they calmly remained standing whenever we passed over. They are, of course, used to aircraft, as the Nairobi–Mombasa flights are routed over this area. They have a long time since become accustomed to the traffic of the railway line and the noise from the trains is as loud and considerably more frequent.

The Yatta Plateau was, from my point of view, the most interesting. At times we could observe several herds of elephant and at least five times we saw a particularly big solitary bull. The tusks were colossal and appeared heavy, as the weight of them gave a rocking movement to his head when walking. Kuhnert* has made a picture of an elephant moving in long yellow grass very much like this one (this picture, by the way, is with Bengt Berg† in Sweden).

One day we observed, in the dense bush between Makindu and Tsavo, a giant of an elephant carrying very long tusks, and not far from this one another big elephant with a single enormous tusk. The biggest of the lot, however, we found on the other side of the Athi, east of Voi. Just then vast herds of elephant could be found in the area, probably as a result of the drought state of the interior bush area, during which the Athi became the only source of water. During this week we must have seen thousands of different elephants. Some herds consisted of a hundred, others of twenty, thirty or fifty animals, and again others of only a few elephants. There were also many towards Kilimanjaro, on the other side of the railway line. This was probably the first time this area had been thoroughly reconnoitered from the air, and we therefore plotted all the waterholes, streams, and potential airstrips on the map. After a month's survey we had gained a good impression of the area and probably knew more about it than our African friends.

Beryl and I obtained great benefit and pleasure from our three months' reconnaissance. I have retained many unforgettable memories from these parts, some of them happy ones when Fortune stood by us and others not so happy, when we would walk in this dry country from sunrise to sunset without finding a single shootable elephant.

I want, however, to tell you about the incident which occurred last week. Dick Cooper and I had planned a month's safari from Makindu to the Yatta Plateau and then on to Malindi, following the Athi down to the sea. There were two reasons for me wanting to do this; the first was an urge to get away from the monotony of farm life and the second was to

*A German big-game painter, especially renowned for his paintings of "the big three"—elephant, lion, and buffalo.
†A naturalist and ornithologist, he accompanied Bror Blixen on several safaris.

get near the big bull that Beryl and I had seen not less than five times when we reconnoitered the area, the bull with the enormous tusks not unlike those depicted in Kuhnert's famous painting.

With us we had Juma, Simba, and Gondo, as well as old Athmani as cook and Abedi functioning as our mess boy. Otherwise we were lightly equipped, with many porters so that in case of need we could carry a water supply for two days. All the porters had light loads which were carried in specially designed rucksacks giving them the use of both hands. In addition, they were equipped with machetes to cut trails through the dense bush. Some parts of the Yatta are overgrown with nasty bush consisting of "wait-a-bit" thorn and bayonet grass. A paradise for elephants, but impenetrable if you are unable to follow the paths made by them or rhino. Of these latter thick-skinned specimens there are plenty about, and if one is obliged to follow their tracks without being able to leave the path, and bearing in mind their disagreeable temper, it is not difficult to imagine that situations such as the one I am about to relate may easily occur. We had not taken out a license for rhino and so as not to distress the elephant we did not want to shoot unless it was absolutely necessary.

Throughout the morning we had been walking in very difficult terrain. The boys had almost incessantly been obliged to cut a passage through the bush. The game paths twisted and bent in multipatterned ways and the heat was infernal. We had seen no elephant and no fresh spoor. Cooper had shot a couple of small buck with his .256 and I had bagged a few francolin for the pot with the shotgun. The boys were exhausted and pouring sweat, their feet sore after walking over the steaming, red-hot ground. At midday we called a halt and rested under a small tree. The boys cleared a space in the bush and put down their loads. Athmani produced the lunch, a couple of camp chairs were erected, and between them a box was put containing a couple of glasses and bottles of gin and lime juice, these being the necessary ingredients for the making of a Tom Collins with which to quench our thirst. There was no view of the surrounding country, as the bush was as dense as a thick hedge. I knew that Kilimanjaro and Maktau should be to our right and Voi straight ahead, i.e., if we had walked in the right direction. I therefore asked one of the boys to climb a small tree and point out the three geographical features to us.

It was nice to sit down after all the creeping and twisting of the morning's walk. The boys stretched and rested their backs against their loads. A bunch of them stood around the water containers, quenching their thirst and passing the snuff boxes between them. The water in the siphon was cool, having been wrapped up in a wet blanket. The rifles, the .22 and the shotgun, were leaning against the trunk of the tree.

The boy aloft pointed to his right, Kilimanjaro and Maktau, and ahead Voi—all as it should be—but, at the same time, informing us that a rhino was approaching along the path where we were just then sitting! The boys jumped up and dispersed, and Simba and Juma began to blow their police whistles, which sometimes causes these living tanks to turn about. We remained calmly seated, thinking that the peacefully strolling monster would be frightened away. Instead, the shrill sound from the whistles made him charge and he came straight at us and our eighty natives. The ground shook under him and he revealed his anger by groaning and puffing. I got hold of the .22 and Cooper reached for the shotgun, and soon after the rhino had initiated his charge I fired, aiming at his horn. Cooper raised his gun and, just as the monster was on him, fired and then fell down behind me, pushed over by the beast. One foot was put through our case of soft drinks and my camp chair was elegantly perched on his horn. Then we waited to see if he was going to turn and renew the attack. Dead silence! No, now the hurricane advanced through the bushes along the path we had just taken. "Are you hurt?" No, nobody had suffered any damage. The gin bottle was in one piece and so was the soda siphon, and only one glass had been broken. The chair which had collapsed could easily be put together again. All of us were somewhat bewildered and we stood still looking at each other until one of us burst out laughing, at which point we all joined in. A hilarious ending to a narrow escape.

In Tsavo we collected our provisions, which had been sent down from Nairobi by train, and the next day we were on our way again. Tsavo—this was the place where, during the construction of the railway in the late 1890s, two man-eating lions had terrorized hundreds of African and Indian workers and within a fairly short space of time killed sixty-four people, including two engineers, before they were finally shot. If you have not read Patterson's description of these days of terror, you should do so. It is called *The Man-eaters of Tsavo* and you can get it in any bookshop in London.

All my love,
Blix

CHAPTER

11

Nairobi

Dear Dick,

Winston has been here for a short visit. As you know, he and his wife have a farm at Mount Kenya, which they wanted to have a look at. Apart from this, he had also asked me to arrange a few days of elephant hunting. This year he has been selected for the national team against England and after this trip he will have to start practicing his polo seriously.

He gave me plenty of notice, so a couple of months before his arrival I got hold of my old friends, Simba, Gondo, and Makula, provisioned them for two months, and instructed them to look separately for big elephants in the Athi River area. On a specific date they were to report telegraphically to me in Nairobi. When the day arrived I received three identically worded telegrams: "Come to M'tito Andei." This railway station is situated halfway between Makindu and Tsavo, and the country all along this stretch consists of fairly dense bush with mainly bayonet grass and thorn trees.

I now had a week before Winston was due to arrive, and so I immediately left for M'tito Andei with fifty boys, tents, provisions, and all the paraphernalia needed for the running of a well-organized camp. I also sent down one of the vehicles belonging to African Guides, as the roads along the railway line are passable during dry season. Our black assistants were immediately given the task of clearing and leveling a field behind the camp which was to be used as a landing strip, as I had engaged Beryl Markham and her plane for a fortnight.

Whilst the clearing was in progress, the three trackers and myself were busy investigating the area and it seemed as if elephant were in plentiful supply. Their tracks were everywhere and we had to reconnoiter very cautiously so as not to disturb them. From time immemorial the big animals have in these desolate areas been disturbed by native ivory hunters, and as soon as they get the wind of humans they leave for other parts of the bush. There is food for them everywhere here, including bayonet grass and certain other species of desert bush which they chew with great relish. They are particularly partial to the cherry-sized berries of a bush somewhat like our deciduous fruit trees, with soft golden-red branches and at this time of year in full bearing. The berries have a faint taste of turpentine. Another bush, rather like a hazel tree, with small thin-skinned fruit, can also be found here. Within the berry there is a kernel and between that and the skin a layer of sweet paste, and although quite small in size they are perhaps the elephants' most appreciated delicacy. The concentration of elephant in the area was almost certainly due to the fact that the berries were now ripe.

Beryl arrived with her aircraft and so inaugurated our 45-by-770-yard-long strip. The surface is firm and level but we shall probably have to increase the length by another fifty-five yards so as to make it more independent of the direction of the wind. We can always land in Tsavo or Makindu and then motor to the camp should wind conditions become too difficult. We made a reconnaissance flight over the elephants at a fair altitude so as not to risk frightening them. A few of them were standing quite close to the railway line by some prominent cliff formations where, now after the rains, there was water in a small pool. There was also plenty of game along the Athi River, as well as to the west of the railway line towards Kilimanjaro. There the country is more open and we saw a big herd of buffalo, many giraffe, as well as other game. Giraffe are easily identified from the air, while the elephant and rhino could be mistaken for antheaps or stony outcrops when at rest.

In the afternoon, Beryl returned to Nairobi in order to fetch Winston the following day. It is hot lately and the air fairly turbulent in the middle of the day, making flying more comfortable in the morning.

By ten o'clock Beryl had already arrived with Winston, having had breakfast in Nairobi. As Simba and Gondo had come in with the news that there were plenty of elephant close to the hills and that they had seen a particularly big bull there, we immediately set forth, taking with us lunch, water, a few blankets in case we should have to stay out overnight, and torches. We walked against an easterly wind, which under the circumstances was ideal. When engaged with elephant hunting, the conditional principles involved are exactly opposite to those prevalent when riding a bicycle. When you go elephant hunting you nearly always find yourself with a following wind and when you bicycle you are usually up against a head wind—both conditions being equally undesirable.

Today, however, luck was with us. Simba had killed a snake in the morning, and Gondo had found a tortoise that had fallen upside down and been able to put it on its legs. He had then fed it with green leaves and, as such things are said to be well rewarded by the deities of the hunt, we therefore walked on in the best of moods.

Winston carried a Gibbs .505, I had a Rigby .416, and in addition we each had a .350 Rigby as second rifles. The grass was dried yellow and fairly short. We followed a dry riverbed with a sandy bottom down towards the hills. A flock of guinea-fowl and a few francolins were having a sand bath in the riverbed but flew away as we approached. The sun blazed down, creating heat waves which followed the wind like ripples on the surface of water. Far away in the distance one could see drifting clouds of smoke from grass fires. High overhead in the blue sky a couple of vultures soared on motionless wings. Their tremendous eyesight had long ago revealed the presence of ourselves and our guns and thereby the possibility of meat and a meal to come. Hour after hour we walked in absolute silence, half asleep in the heat. The brain improvises in such conditions, indulging in daydreams as when you are only half-awake.

Suddenly Simba, who walks in front, stops and we wake up. He gives us a warning. We are close to the hills—better to proceed without any noise. We steal forward more carefully and, now completely alert, start climbing the hot rugged cliffside. Below us we can see a thorn tree standing by the edge of a small pool and completely covered with the nests of weaver birds. Elephant have brought down a couple of old trees which now lie dried up and dead with their roots pointing skywards. The blue and wet clay along the edges of the pool indicates that the elephants have been drinking there not so many hours ago and the nearby bushes are sprayed with mud. Presently we hear a thud from the thicket—a tree has been brought down—and a little later we see red earth being thrown up in the air. So now we know where the elephants are.

We leave the superfluous boys on the hill and continue with Simba, Gondo, Makula, and Juma Nandi. There is an easterly crosswind blowing and the elephants are due north from us, and we therefore make a detour westwards. Every now and then we hear them. A dull crack when the big ears smack against their bodies, a puff when they shower their backs with sand—but we are still too far away to discern the characteristic tummy rumblings. We advance slowly and in absolute silence. By the different sounds we must try to estimate the distance and number of the animals, but as they are now having their siesta, there is no particular hurry. We are approaching upwind when we suddenly hear a heavy thud not so far away. One of the elephants has brought down a tree in order to get at the tender top branches. We steal forward in that direction—and there we see two elephants standing with their heads buried in the treetop, one on each side. The one on the right side carries two tusks of some ninety lbs., the other one rather poor. We withdraw cautiously as we want to have a good look at them all before making up our minds, and this has to be done one step at a time. A broken twig can warn them, and if they cross our tracks or get our wind—they'll be off.

Now we hear another couple further ahead. We cannot approach them head-on as an odd gust of wind might bring our scent to the others, so we shall have to make a detour to our left. All our senses are at full alert and the muscles under control—no stones must be dislodged, no twigs broken. Another one appears, a bull with his tail towards us, so we cannot see his tusks. Further to the left yet another one can be glimpsed and behind him several animals can be heard puffing and blowing. To approach closer would be risky, because if the nearest elephants got our wind they would immediately rush off and take the entire herd with them. We therefore cautiously withdraw a short distance, sit down, and discuss a suitable plan of procedure.

Having deliberated a few minutes, we finally agree that Winston and I, with Juma and Gondo, should go back to the first elephants, and there within shooting range await Simba and Makula, who are to go further ahead in an effort to get a look at the others. If those that are nearest then get their wind, there will still be enough time for us to shoot the big bull.

We estimate it will take about ten minutes for us to get there and so we sneak away in the same direction. The elephants have moved a short distance, but we are soon there and position ourselves by a tree somewhat bigger than the first. The sun is beating down on our shoulders and backs. A couple of banded mongoose about the size of our shrews, with pretty yellow stripes along the body, run about around the base of the nearest bush. They don't take the slightest notice of us, but every time one of the elephants blows dust over himself the mongooses sit up and look in that direction only to continue their search for food as soon as the noise has stopped. The shadow of a soaring vulture floats along the ground and we unintentionally look up to where he glides on taut motionless wings with eyes focused and beak pointed towards the ground.

Suddenly something happens. The elephant to the right lifts up his trunk, sniffing the air, and the other one does the same. A deep rumbling indicates that they have noticed something suspicious and are ill at ease. The tips of their trunks are probing in all directions—this abominable scent, could it come from a human being? No, the trunks come down again, but we can see that they are extremely alert and prepared to rush off at any moment. One of them is standing with his right leg raised, just resting the tip of his foot on the ground, his ears stretched like gale-filled sails. Then a gust of wind brings the scent of our scouts and at the same moment they rush in headlong flight straight at us. I hurriedly whisper to Winston to fire at the shoulder of the big bull at the first available chance, and before the words are out of my mouth they come crashing past. Winston fires and the elephants disappear, but the others from the high ground above follow and Winston gets a shot at the nearest one. This one falls just ahead of us, dragging with him a tree. Further beyond comes a giant with tusks like thick branches and I just have time to point him out so that Winston can get in a shot and I can also fire. Then everything is quiet; it is all over in a flash. What has really happened? In front of us there is a young bull with smallish tusks and another two animals have been shot at. We shall have to wait until all the trackers have gathered together and arrived.

We start tracking the elephant that had first been wounded and the spoor shows a lot of blood. Simba leads, followed by myself, with Winston just behind. The vegetation around us consists of bayonet grass and thick shrub, and we advance cautiously until we hear a thud followed by a shrill trumpet blast. We have all stopped and Simba whispers in my ear, "Nakufa." Well, we now all know he is dead, and when we reach the spot we see him stretched out on his side. The tusks are really good, of an even length, and thicker than we had thought. We then go back to the other tracks and after a bit of searching find the spoor of the one we had both been firing at. Simba, possibly the best tracker in Africa, sets out in front with the rest of us following in single file. Everybody is greatly keyed up, as there has been no evidence of blood and we have a following wind behind us. This is not to our advantage, but we have to follow the spoor. Then, suddenly, the trail double backs; he was probably alerted when the other one fell. He must be badly wounded not to have continued his flight.

We are now tracking against prevailing wind and are presently aware of a strong smell of elephant, and some fifty paces away I can see a probing trunk raised above the bushes. We increase the speed of our advance and soon see a gray mass moving forward. A few more steps and we hear him. It sounds like water against the sides of a ship when he glides through dense vegetation. Then he enters a small glade and we can see him between two bushes. With the speed of a practiced hunter Winston fires, and the bull falls as if the legs had been knocked out from under him, there to remain with head and trunk thrown back. Life has gone—a bullet has severed his spine.

It was a magnificent bull and we guessed his tusks would weigh out at about a hundred and thirty lbs. each and the other one at about a hundred lbs. These estimates later proved to be absolutely right. You can imagine that Beryl was extremely pleased, as this was the first result of the reconnaissance in which we had been so much engaged.

The game department was good enough not to include in their quote the small elephant that Winston had been forced to shoot, but naturally they kept the tusks.

One day when Winston had to go into town, Beryl expressed a wish to see elephant at closer quarters, having seen so many from the air. She also wanted to get some photos of them all by herself. As the morning was bright and sunny we decided to take the plane in order to locate a suitable camera subject within reasonable walking distance of our tents.

We were still camped at M'tito Andei, with the aircraft only a few yards away, and all we had to do was top up the oil. I swung the propeller, three turns backwards, one forward, and the kind engine came to life. Five minutes of idling, a few revving tests, and we were taxiing down to the north end of the strip. The sun was just coming up over the horizon when we cleared the treetops against a southerly morning breeze. We rose slowly to an altitude of 1,000 feet, circled the landing strip, and skimmed over the bush. We followed the railway line eastwards and watched the icy blue dome of Kilimanjaro gradually being tinted rose by the rising sun. The air was clear after the cool night, but along the riverbeds one could see veils of white mist floating along, finally fading away before the increasingly hot sunshine.

We saw two lions sunning themselves down by the cliffs where we had followed the elephants. Flocks of vultures lifted off from the trees, which indicated that there were still remnants from the carcasses. We gained altitude by banking repeatedly, the wind played tunes on the struts, the engine hummed, and it was wonderful to be alive. Quite close to the Imperial Airways landing strip at Makindu we spotted a small herd of elephant totaling about ten animals. Here the country was easy and open, and a path which I knew of by previous walking in the area would take us up to the place where the elephants were standing.

We landed, put canvas covers over propeller and engine, and asked the airfield personnel to keep watch over the Avian. A few natives who had heard the plane and seen it landing came running along, and I engaged two to carry my rifle, camera, lunch, and water bottles. It took us a couple of hours to reach the place. Great baobab trees dotted the landscape, which otherwise consisted of dense bush with thorn trees and bayonet grass. To me these giant baobabs do not quite look real, and are no more similar to other trees than the giraffe and rhino resemble other animals. Close to Makindu we got through cultivated land, and to start with the path wound from hut to hut between neat little fields of maize, millet, and bananas. Inquisitive children stared at us, mongrels barked by huts, and lots of stray chicken and goats could be seen everywhere.

It was now getting hot, but we were beginning to get close. From the air we had noted that there were some cliffs and big thorn trees close to where the elephants were standing. When our porters were told this they immediately understood where the place was. The wind was fairly favorable—northeasterly—and the elephants would now be to the east of us. Soon we heard some trumpeting—first contact—so it seemed likely that there would be some cows and calves amongst them. After a while we heard all the familiar sounds—the flapping of ears, the puffing when blowing dust, and the flop of droppings falling to the ground.

The area in which they were standing was covered with dense vegetation which did not make photography easy, and it would probably be difficult to get a good clear picture of them. Beryl had a Leica with telephoto lens, and the most suitable distance ought to have been thirty-five to forty-five yards. However, the animals were still feeding and in motion, so there was a chance they would get out of the heavy bush and walk over to another clump of trees a little to our right. In all there seemed to be about a dozen elephants. We moved slowly to the next thicket, and there under a big baobab we awaited further developments. I carried my .350 Rigby, but as neither of us had a license I could not use it if at all avoidable.

After a wait of some fifteen minutes, a big bull came out and walked diagonally towards the thicket on our right, which would be ideal for distance when he passed a small clearing through which the path would lead him. I told Beryl to take him the moment he emerged on the path.

When he crossed it there would be a chance he would get our wind and then he would probably turn around and rush off, taking all the others with him.

He really looked majestic as he approached. The big thick tusks caused his head to swing slowly up and down in rhythm with his pace. He was chewing on some bayonet grass and was clearly enjoying the sun on his broad back. Then he was on the path and the Leica clicked. He checked for a moment but continued, and then he got our wind. But instead of going back, as I had thought he would, he turned straight towards us with ears pricked; he evidently meant business! "Run back, all of you," I shouted at the same moment as he charged, his trunk stretched out, ears extended, and the small piggy eyes gleaming with rage. I remained by the tree, prepared to shoot if necessary. Just before he was on me, he stopped, emitted two triumphant trumpet blasts, turned around, and ambled back to his family, leaving behind a comical impression of satisfaction. The enemy had been frightened away; he had done his duty! Beryl was delighted. "By Jove, I've never been so frightened in my life."

We walked back to Makindu, started the engine, and, as it was only midday, decided to take a trip to Malindi for a swim. A refreshing dip, a good lunch, and a laze on the beach listening to the swell of the ocean is not a bad way of whiling away a few hours.

The beautiful horseshoe-shaped bay at Malindi has an ideal bathing beach. The sand is soft and clean and the breakers slowly roll in over shallow waters where the coral reef keeps the sharks at bay. The wind whispers in the coconut palms and the air is permeated with the smell of salt water, fish, and seaweed. The sea is as blue as the sky above, in which the gulls on their white wings soar over the breakers.

We flew back that evening, and Winston returned on the eight o'clock train. In front of an enormous campfire we recounted the day's adventures. Winston had brought letters and newspapers, oranges and pineapples had arrived from Zanzibar, and ice from Mombasa. The cool drinks tasted magnificent, the stars twinkled, and in the west a new moon smiled pleasantly at us, promising good weather for the next day.

Yours ever,
Blix

CHAPTER
12

Nairobi

Dear Dick,

Now I am going to relate a piece of the most extraordinary luck I have had, how, within the reaches of civilization, I have for my client managed to get elephants bigger than anything than I myself have walked hundreds of miles to get.

Freddie Guest is here with his daughter Diana, and he wanted to have a week's elephant hunt with her. I had previously engaged Simba, Gondo, and Makula as permanent trackers and through them I knew that there were plenty of elephant between Maungu railway station and Mount Kasigau, which is situated as a final outpost overlooking the dry, waterless plains below the Paré Mountains. Kasigau is an imposing cone of granite and an outstanding landmark. There is a wood on the north side, but otherwise it is almost completely bare. At the foot of the mountain there is a small permanent stream with beautiful crystal-clear water.

During the dry season elephants come there whenever they want to refresh themselves with really good water. Otherwise they are able to stay without for weeks, as in this area there is a plentiful supply of the juicy sansevieria, or bayonet grass, with its fleshy spiked leaves which the elephant chews and extracts his requirement of liquid from. I have often hunted here but never been particularly lucky. Simba and Gondo, however, consider this the best of all hunting grounds for big game.

Last year, in order to get a truck through from Maungu to Kasigau, I cut a track out of the bush, and along this there is a series of hillocks, mostly covered by thick bush, and in the gorges between these it is practically impossible to get through. The impressive massif of Kilimanjaro can be seen seventy miles southwest of here and then there is the long range of the Paré Mountains the whole way down to the coast. There is plenty of game. Buffalo and lion are numerous, and, worse luck, also rhino—in this type of country not desirable, particularly as we are not after them. A lot of oryx, zebra, Grant's gazelle, and an unusual amount of lesser kudu and gerenuk. One also often sees the long necks of giraffe sticking up above the surrounding bush.

I sent our equipment by truck two days in advance to a point about three miles from Maungu, where camp was made. I had engaged thirty porters in Voi, but the camp boys were the usual ones. My friend and partner Philip Percival was coming with us so that we could hunt in two different directions at the same time.

The four of us (Freddie, Diana, Philip, and I) took the afternoon train from Nairobi, had dinner aboard, and arrived at Maungu in the night, where we were met by the waiting vehicles. In camp, fires were lit in front of the tents and the staff assembled to greet the guests. Simba and his colleagues were very optimistic, but in spite of this we decided to rest in the morning and use the day for a reconnaissance trip to Kasigau by car.

As always this time of year, the morning was extremely beautiful. At eight o'clock we all had breakfast together and packed our requirements for the day in two cars—food, water, and porters with axes and spades in case the road should be blocked. It was now a long time since a vehicle had passed there, and it appears to be a favorite pastime of the elephant to push a tree across a man-made road in the same way that the ant bear likes to make his holes along whatever narrow passage we intend to travel.

There were plenty of elephant tracks, and we stopped and inspected all those that crossed the road. Halfway there we found some deep depressions in the rock and there was still some water in them after the last rains. The elephants like this place, as they are the only ones that can get at the water with their long trunks. The tracks showed that four bulls had been drinking there during the night. Simba, full of enterprise, was all for starting tracking them at once, but as we had agreed to use this day for reconnaissance only, we carried on. The closer we got to Kasigau, the more spoor we found; all the elephants from the Paré range seemed to have arranged a meeting here. We arrived at the mountain at midday, after having had to cut our way through the bush in several places.

Simba, who was standing behind me, suddenly pushed me in the back and told me to stop moving. He pointed up towards the mountainside; there a row of elephants was wandering up towards some big boulders. Completely undisturbed, they sauntered slowly on and by the boulders more animal backs could be seen. One stood poised on top of a cliff and his big white tusks were gleaming in the sun. He was about a mile away. We quickly held a council of war and it was decided that Diana and I together with our gunbearers should try and get up to the cliffs, whilst Freddie and Philip were to remain behind awaiting further developments. Should the elephants get our wind and turn, the others, with their car, might be able to cut them off on their way down to the plains.

It was hot now and the excitement made us still warmer. The gradient up the mountain began to tell. Our pulse raced more quickly and we urged each other to take it easy, forever more easy! On our side of the big boulder stood a single bull. We had to get to the highest point, at whatever sacrifice in time and labor—from there we would get a good view of all the elephants and be able to choose the biggest one for our target. Just then the wind was in our favor, but on mountain slopes it is generally unreliable; it can be sucked upwards or a strong gust can direct it towards the side of the mountain in an instant. Still, we had to proceed forward; the chance would have to be taken.

Now the elephant walks behind the cliffs. The way is clear and we hurry on. Ahead, by the cliffs, we hear many elephants; their ears are flapping against their sides and cascades of earth are flying over the bushes as we listen to their puffing and blowing. The cliffs are formed like an amphitheater, with the highest furthest away. The best way to get there appears to be to follow the bed of a small dried-out rivulet. The animals can be heard to the right of the crags, but they are moving and we follow on their heels. Simba goes in front and gives Diana a helping hand over the steepest parts, with me pushing from behind and followed by Gondo, who in his turn shoves me along.

Now we are up. The summit is bare and flat like a floor. Below us there is a valley crowned with fairly thick bush and on the other side still another bare cliff. The elephants are now moving towards the right, heading for the gully, which is about a hundred and fifty feet deep. The closest elephants are just between us and there are many of them! The broad backs form a movable gray mass. What a wonderful sight! I have never seen anything more impressive. I count twenty-five elephants, all bulls and all within range of less than a hundred yards. "Take it easy, Diana," I urge. "Be prepared in case the wind changes direction. When they start moving, shoot at the one I will point out to you, but I still don't know which is the biggest." Many are big and Simba indicates one whose tusks I estimate to be about a hundred lbs. Then a still bigger one emerges a little to the left and further behind. They walk down towards the valley with the biggest farthest behind. Diana now understands which one I mean. Soon the leading animals will get our wind and then they will all move off. "Aim at the shoulder, but not yet. He'll get nearer, but don't take your eyes off him." The entire herd is now on the move, with the old one still bringing up the rear and not more than sixty yards away. Diana is completely calm and prepared to fire.

Suddenly the leader's trunk is raised, then another one follows suit. The first few speed up their walk and the rest do the same. "Fire, Diana!" We hear the dull echo from the crack of the rifle which travels from mountaintop to mountaintop. The elephants disappear in a cloud of dust, trees are broken and pulled down, boulders are loosened and roll down into the gully, trumpet blasts are sounded—the noise is indescribable! I get another glimpse of the big one lying with all four legs under him and his heavy body resting against a palm tree. We can now see the remainder in a long row; in their peculiar gliding jog-trot they are hurrying out to the plains, crossing the motor road not more than two hundred yards from Freddie and Philip.

We wave from the cliff and then get down into the gulley. The bull was very good, the best I've seen for a long time. Before the tusks are taken out it is difficult to estimate their weight. The reason for this is that the upper part of the tusk is hollow, containing a pulpy substance which in turn protects the main nerve. The length of this cavity varies considerably—from six inches to over three feet—and obviously affects the weight. Diana offered ten shillings for the best guess. When in the evening the tusks were put on the station master's scales the weights turned out to be 125 and 126 lbs. respectively, and Gondo became the winner.

The vehicles could almost reach the fallen elephant, and by that time it was half past one. Chairs were put up under a tree, the luncheon basket was placed on a flat slab of rock, bottles of beer were cooled around the ice container, and presently a good lunch was eaten whilst the boys were chopping out the tusks. To do this without damaging the ivory is a skilled job and generally takes five to six hours to accomplish. Now, however, it took much less time, as the animal was so placed that the men could work from both sides simultaneously. In the meantime others were cutting out special titbits from the carcass. The entire trunk was removed and placed on one of the trucks, but it took four men to carry it. In the cavity at the root of the trunk there is a cartilaginous layer of fat which is supposed to be a great delicacy and this was of course carefully scraped out. An entire foreleg and a big slice from the back were also removed.

The view towards the Paré Mountains, with Kilimanjaro in the background, is spectacular. Unfortunately, on this occasion a cloud hid most of the summit, but one still got a glimpse of the snow below it. We got back just as the sun was going down. Just before we reached the camp Freddie shot a very good lesser kudu in a glade. Abedi butchered it in the correct Muslim way to ensure that it would not only be the infidels that had meat in their pots that night.

The hunt had started well, Diana had got—as far as I know—the biggest elephant any woman had ever shot, and in addition all of us had had the rare opportunity to enjoy the sight of twenty-five elephants—all with tusks over one hundred lbs.—descending the mountainslope before entering the thick all-concealing bush. At this point there must be a lot of elephants on the plains, as so many bulls have elected to separate from the "madding crowd." During the war Philip Percival was commanding the forces that were stationed here to prevent the Germans from sabotaging the railway line. He told me how he had deployed his men, and how in spite of all vigilance enemy patrols sometimes succeeded in infiltrating, causing bridges to be blown and rolling stock to be destroyed. All the country around Kasigau was then under cultivation, but because of the threat from spies and bribed African guides, the entire population was moved. Since then the elephants have moved in.

That night I slept well. There are a lot of hazards involved in elephant hunting and one can never promise or be sure of anything. Should we not see another elephant, this trip would still have been considered successful.

The sun rose in a glowing blaze next morning and Philip came to meet me by the campfire outside my tent. Abedi came running with chairs and a small table, and so we sat down to make our plans for the day. Two steaming cups of tea with some ginger and cheese biscuits is not a bad first breakfast. The first rays of sunshine sent white mists through the valley and along the slopes of the hills in a billowy veil-dance; the last shadows from the night were being driven away. Softly padding messboys entered the guest tents with the tea trays.

It was obvious that most of the interest would have to be centered on Daddy Freddie, who yesterday had had no opportunity with elephant. Makula, who while our hunt was in progress had been out reconnoitering behind Nyangala Hill (by Maungu, and where we were camped), reported that he had seen three big bulls and did not think that they had been in any way disturbed by our shooting, as he himself had heard nothing of either shots or noise from the cars. That the natives had been singing and rejoicing by the flesh pots during the night did not matter, as the elephants were used to such noises so close to the railway station.

We decided that Philip, Makula, Simba, and the required number of porters should go with Freddie, and that Diana and myself should go in the same direction as yesterday. It was possible we might find fresh tracks again.

It doesn't take long to get dressed in Africa. One has one's bath in the evening, as the hot water helps to take the stiffness away from tired legs and feet. The bacon and eggs and the good Kenya coffee for breakfast were finished quickly.

We said good-bye to Freddie and his party and seated ourselves in the car, where the men were already installed with all the things we were taking along, and so we slowly started down the road, or more correctly, the track. There was still dew in the shade of the bushes and the ground was dark with moisture.

We got onto the first spoor quite close to the big waterhole in the cliffs, twelve miles from camp. That was the one we examined yesterday and found that three bulls had been drinking there. I myself didn't think the tracks were particularly big, but Gondo was very enthusiastic. "One of them is the one that got away at the time when *Mtoto ya Kingi* was here," he said, very sure of himself. *Mtoto ya Kingi* (son of the king) was the Prince of Wales. We got out, left the car and driver, and started tracking. We were now walking due south and the wind was from the north, so conditions couldn't have been worse. However, Gondo was stubborn and wanted to continue. "They are not very close yet," he said. "They are on the other side of that hill. When we get as far as that the sun will be overhead and the afternoon breeze always comes from the northwest," so we ambled on.

You could only walk in the tracks, as the sansevieria was flattened and trampled down there and one would have been repeatedly pricked by its spikes. Nevertheless it was strenuous walking. One had to be on the alert all the time. If one happens to tread on one of the spikes, it can penetrate the sole of a shoe. The popular name "bayonet grass" is indicative of the damage it will cause when coming in contact with any part of the human body. It has been known to blind a man forever. You have probably seen them in other areas, a sporadic plant here and there, but around Kasigau they grow as densely as reeds. The natives also call them "the forts of the elephant," a very appropriate expression. So this is why we had to proceed so slowly.

The sun climbed higher, gradually it became hotter, and the contents of the water bottles warmer. I glanced at Diana's face, which had become pinker. "Go on, old boy, I'm okay!" Personally, I did not have much hope for today's hunt. Yesterday had been so lucky and successful that a repeat performance seemed impossible. Gondo, however, was still on his toes and optimistic. He held an old sock in his hands half filled with flour, which he shook periodically to determine the direction of the wind. Suddenly he stopped, sniffed, and shook his sock. "Now the wind has turned and it will blow from this direction for the rest of the afternoon." Behind the mountain the terrain is more open and nothing like as dense as where we were. "By the time it is four o'clock the bulls will graze there," he added with great conviction. Optimism always helps. The heat was now suffocating and every step was an effort. Admittedly, the gunbearers walked in front and with their razor-sharp bush knives cut the worst sansevieria leaves, but even so we couldn't avoid being pricked now and then.

Suddenly, without anybody having expected it, we heard the familiar sound of elephant ears flapping against a body and then some puffing, probably not more than a hundred yards away. All fatigue immediately vanished. Gondo carries my .505 and Juma Diana's .350. Gondo leads, then myself, Juma, and Diana. We produce our secateurs, the only instrument I know of that can silently cut off sansevieria and protruding branches. The wind remains steady and we creep slowly and carefully forward. Now we hear more flapping of the ears, and the occasional snorting seems to indicate he is half asleep. We are now so near that we can hear the protests from the swarms of insects as they are swept away by the enormous ears. A few steps more, extremely slowly and with bodies perfectly balanced. A gray shadow moves over there, slightly to our left. I shove Gondo to the side, push Diana in front of me, and take over her .350. Gondo is now behind me.

Any moment now the elephant should start coming in our direction. But he just stands there feeling safe within his fortress, to which there is no direct access. It is not yet four o'clock. Isn't he soon going to start grazing down in the glade? The terrain couldn't be worse; it is practically impossible to take a step to either side. Our way ahead looks like a description from the Middle Ages of a path of horror where the victim is forced to pass between rows of spears. Suddenly I realize that this is the worst possible place imaginable to take a young girl elephant hunting. How on earth could I have let myself get involved in a situation like this? I curse Gondo, silently but sincerely.

Now he moves again over there. He showers earth over neck and shoulders with his trunk and when he throws his head back he exposes a most magnificent pair of tusks high above the surrounding grass. All self-accusation immediately vanishes, life is beautiful and glorious, and Gondo is the most excellent man alive.

We are now only twenty-five yards from him, but the grass is very thick. In front of us and to the left there is a small tree exactly in the direction he is now taking. "High on the shoulder, when you see him," I whisper, and hand her the .350 with the safety catch off. At the same time I automatically receive my rifle from Juma.

Diana knows exactly where to aim. We have sketched this on paper every night. She has only once been nervous, and that was when she thought she might not be allowed to come on this safari.

Now the tusks emerge from the bushes, there comes the head, and then the forelegs. *Bang*. With a heavy sigh the giant sinks to the ground with a broken back and folding hindlegs. But a fallen elephant can get up again, and we wait with rifles at the ready. Then comes the drawn-out trumpet call signaling the end. *"Nakufa."* He is dead.

We had to cut our way through the scrub and sansevieria to get to him. The tusks were colossal, bigger than those of the day before. Gondo was jubilant and everybody shook hands. Then the tip of the tail was cut off, the trophy which is required from all native elephant hunters as evidence that he really has killed. Without it he won't be believed. Bracelets are made from the hair and presented to the hunter's best girl.

To get out of that place was almost more difficult than to enter. This was partly because we were now in a hurry to get back to camp and partly because we did not have a newly trodden elephant track to follow. We had to cut down everything ourselves with secateurs and bush knives. However, after two hours's hard work we were on the car track and half an hour later we reached the vehicle. The others had not returned yet, but shots had been heard by the people in the camp. Abedi was very pleased when he saw the tail and heard about the size of the tusks. The cook, Athmani, turned up with his staff and immediately wanted to arrange for a war dance, but we were longing for tea and hot baths, so the dancing would have to be postponed till the evening.

I was completely amazed by the events of the day and could hardly believe that they had really happened. If yesterday's tusks had weighed a hundred and twenty lbs., those of today most surely have weighed at least a hundred and thirty lbs. For months I had been wandering through the primeval forests of Uganda and the Congo and in vain searched for a really big elephant, then along comes an English miss and in two days bags these giants! Naturally I was immensely pleased, but couldn't help wonder whether the goddess of Fate is always completely impartial.

We had our most welcome hot baths and then Abedi had to give me a stiff whisky and soda to help me get over these happenings and make me look calm and unimpressed by the time the others returned.

It was late by the time Philip and Freddie came back. We had placed a hurricane lamp in the top of a thorn tree and also had Verey lights, but didn't have to use them. Both of them were very dusty and tired. The camp chair creaked when old Freddie relaxed in it. "Well, Blix," he said. "I've shot a bloody big elephant and had to fire at another one that nearly trampled me down, but that one we haven't been able to find."

Well, of course our different experiences that day had to be swapped; the tea and hot baths removed their tiredness and presently the great campfire promoted the right atmosphere of relaxed content. The song of the natives behind the kitchen, the tinkle of ice in the silver cooler, comfortable chairs—all this combined in making the evening unforgettable.

Next morning Diana caught the train back to Nairobi and we three men stayed on. She, of course, had had all her wishes fulfilled and now wanted to tell her friends all that she had experienced in the way of excitement and luck in the course of those two eventful days.

We followed the schedule of the first day and decided on a day of reconnaissance. The tusks had to be taken out of the elephants we had got the previous day and there would be a certain amount of commotion all over the area. The wind would carry the smell of carrion out over the plains, and the game would be scared off. Better to investigate the conditions in another direction. In addition to our faithful trackers we took half a dozen natives with us and started off in our trucks. We took both of them to reduce the risk of a breakdown, which can become unpleasant in this type of country that is so far from any supply of spares.

Just before coming to Kasigau, where we the first day had seen all the bulls, we had to cross a small dried-out riverbed. Here three bulls had recently passed. That they all three were bulls we could read from their spoor. They had been walking towards the plains from the direction the wind was blowing—why not follow them? What their tusks were like we wouldn't know until we had seen them.

It was fairly open there, not like the dense bush and sansevieria through which Diana and I had had to penetrate the previous day. After a couple of miles along this riverbed one gets to some cliff formations, and the tracks led towards these. The time was by then nearly eleven o'clock and it was beginning to get hot. Freddie, who was over sixty, was not anxious to have another strenuous day like the day before, so we climbed the cliffs with the intention of taking a siesta somewhere in the shade. Just on the other side, however, stood a small herd of elephants of which we could only discern their backs and ears. Evidently these animals had not been disturbed by the events of the previous day, as they were standing tranquilly, half asleep.

I suggested that Freddie and Philip should stay put whilst I went down to investigate if any of them were worth shooting.

The first I came across were cows and calves, about twenty of them, and further on there were five smallish bulls. I climbed a tree to get a wider view. My efforts were richly rewarded and another three-quarters of a mile away I discovered three big bulls. At that distance it was difficult to make an accurate estimate of their ivory, but they appeared big and well worth closer investigation. It was by then past one o'clock, so I went back to the others and we all continued carefully, avoiding the herd, in the direction I had seen the three bulls. It took us over an hour, and when we got there the elephants had left. Their spoor, however, were easy to follow in the sand and so the stealthy tracking which one has described so often in connection with elephants—always exciting, frequently dangerous—commenced again.

Two of the animals were slowly walking forward, one had stopped. Simba was sent ahead to investigate what kind of ivory he was carrying, and after a while returned to report that he had no tusks at all. This seemed to me strange and very unusual in these parts, so I decided to go in and have a look at this phenomenon. As the wind was coming from my left I took a detour to the right, and presently I saw one big tusk. Leaning forward I saw the tip of another tusk and beckoned to the others to proceed cautiously.

He had his backside towards us, but a bullet just above the root of his tail would break his back and a second one behind the ear would painlessly end his life. And so it happened. Freddie put him down with his big .505 and I did the rest—which probably wasn't even necessary—with my .416.

He was magnificent. Philip and I looked at each other, and Freddie rubbed his hands. "Boy, oh boy, send for the trucks to the nearest gettable place and we'll take this evening's train to Nairobi! The staff and tusks can follow later. Tonight we are going to celebrate."

This, at least in recent years, is probably the most successful three-day elephant hunt to have occurred. The safari with all equipment, tusks, and the entire staff was back in Nairobi on the sixth day after setting out with four pairs of tusks averaging 115 lbs. apiece.

After that hunt the silhouette of Mount Kasigau will always be a welcome and memorable sight to me, and happy memories are the spice of life.

Yours ever,
Blix

CHAPTER
13

· ·

London
June 1936

My darling Eva,

I am now in London, more than a month ahead of schedule, and in a
few days' time I will be in Stockholm. The reason for this is that Beryl
Markham, who knew that I was on the point of leaving for home, asked
me in Nairobi if I would like to fly with her to England instead of taking a
boat—she had as a lone woman been refused clearance to fly over the
Sudan and so had to have a man with her. This suited me to perfection,
and three days later we were on our way. Flo,* Betty,† and Dicky
Crofton‡ wanted to see us off and went with us to the airfield, where
heavy mists delayed our departure for more than half an hour. Soon,
however, we got a glimpse of the Kikuyu Escarpment and, with a favorable tail wind, took off for Kisumu, our first intermediate landing. It is a
beautiful flight and, having skimmed over the Escarpment at low altitude,
one is overwhelmed by an odd sensation when the mountains suddenly
disappear and one gets a first glimpse of the Kedong Valley two thousand
feet below. In the strong light from the morning sun the furrowed slopes
of the craters stood out like faces of old men and lakes Naivasha, Elemen-
teita, and Nakuru glittered like enormous mirrors as we flew over them.
West of the Rift wall the landscape consists mostly of broken highlands
intersected by picturesque valleys, but after that the terrain becomes mo-

---

*Florence Crofton: Dick Crofton's wife, daughter of General Northey, the previous gov-
ernor of Kenya.
†Flo's daughter by a previous marriage.
‡A white hunter who often acted as Bror Blixen's second-in-command on safaris. He was
one of the first casualties in East Africa in World War II.

notonous. We made a sweep over Murchison Falls at the head of the White Nile, of which I retain many pleasant memories.

We filled up with petrol in Juba and immediately after a light lunch continued to Khartoum, where we arrived at five o'clock. This stage is tedious, taking you over flat, almost desert-like country the whole way. Every so often we would follow the Nile, but here the river winds its way in and out of a straight compass bearing pointing due north. Dust devils were sucked skywards by gusts of wind and appeared like compact pillars rising from the desert floor. We flew at a fair altitude in order to avoid the heat, and the scorched ground below us could only hazily be discerned.

Even Khartoum looked dead and deserted. Camels were being driven in single file over flat fields, and a few vehicles were causing sand and dust to rise into the air. At the airport, however, there was great activity. On the runways there were several Italian aircraft intended for the Abyssinian campaign, as well as British squadrons with their bivouacked crews prepared for any emergency. The hotel was full of uniformed officers, all of them discussing war, the United Nations, neutrality, and the affront to Abyssinia. I could not help thinking of our friend Haile Selassie, who had done so much to help us when we were there together only a few months ago. What would now happen to him? And to Ras Desta, who had ordered crow's nests to be built in the treetops so his snipers could engage the Italian Air Force with ordinary Mauser rifles! Should these people really be forced into war against a superior white power? Could the United Nations allow such a thing?

As already mentioned, Khartoum was full of the military and uniforms could be seen everywhere. We got rooms, however, and that evening I went to see Pongo Barker, the game warden, and after a walk in his pleasant zoological garden we discussed game laws and game protection over a sun-downer on his cool veranda.

I cannot remember if you have seen his zoo. It is in reality only a big park with palms and fig trees where the animals roam freely about— gazelles and antelopes of various species and birds of the Sudanese fauna, from *abu markub* and crested cranes to weavers and honey birds. There were elephant, rhinos, giraffes, monkeys, lions, and leopards behind protective barriers. Everything was enclosed with pleasing fences running along the boundaries of the big park. A really magnificent piece of work achieved by a true nature lover who had had very limited resources at his disposal.

We started at dawn the following morning. The weather was calm and the engine was humming pleasantly in the cool morning breeze. At first we followed the Nile, but after an hour's flight we left the river, and two and a half hours later we reached Wadi Halfa. This is where you leave the Sudan and enter Egyptian territory, and so have to clear documents before being allowed to continue.

While this was being done and our passports stamped, we drove up to the small hotel situated in a pleasant garden by the shores of the Nile and there we were able to breakfast on bacon, eggs and coffee.

Presently we were off again. At times we followed the Nile and at times we flew over the desert, its scorching sand glowing below us. By the middle of the day it was getting bumpy and extremely hot, and the dust devils mounted skywards for hundreds of yards. A tiresome day, and when we reached Luxor at about five o'clock we decided to stay the night. Having filled up with petrol and oil and parked the plane in a small shed, we traveled into town by car. It was nice to get a cool drink after the long day—a bath, dinner, and then early to bed. We had great difficulty making the hotel staff understand that we wanted separate rooms. Our declaration that we were not married made no impression on them; they just kept on assuring us that they had a so beautiful double room with a view of the river and a private balcony and bathroom! When I insisted on two rooms with baths, it was not until I added, "I snore," that I got full understanding and sympathy.

At this time of the year Luxor was fairly free of tourists and therefore comparatively quiet and peaceful. The drowsy murmurings of the palm fronds, the encouraging calls from the donkey drivers in the distance, the organ grinders on some street corners and the monotonous singsong of women's voices down below all contributed to soon lulling one to sleep.

We were called at four-thirty the next morning. We wanted to be in Cairo early so as to give the plane a thorough overhaul and thought this would take a couple of days. It would probably also be necessary to acquire clearances to fly over Libya, Tunisia, and Sardinia before going on to Nice as planned.

As you know, spring in Cairo is warm. Beryl had a lot of air-minded friends there and she spent most of her time with them. I also went out for dinner and drinks with people I knew and visited a number of museums and art galleries. When viewing Tutankhamen's collected treasures and works of art one became, of course, completely overwhelmed with admiration.

It took exactly eight days to obtain clearance for the various documents required, but by then the engine was like new and everything had been checked. The small aircraft shone and glittered in the sunshine.

At seven A.M. we took off from Heliopolis. A couple of friends from the RAF had turned up to see us off and they followed us, providing escort over the townships of Cairo, the fertile Nile delta, and the pyramids, which at this time were rose-tinted by the morning sun.

The compass bearing was set towards Mersa Matrûh, where we estimated, with this comparatively slow aircraft, we would arrive in two hour's flying time. Below us the shadow of the Leopard Moth passed over ditches, sand ridges, and fertile fields—always fascinating to watch—and I speculated on how it would feel to rush along on the ground at the same speed.

We flew over what may well be the world's most fertile area, covered by silt from the mysterious river Nile, which carried earth from the Mountains of the Moon and the Abyssinian Highlands and water from lakes Victoria, Edward, and Albert, then flowed in a long, wide, and yellow stream through the great scorching desert. The people live here in the same way as they have for thousands of years, and we could observe the fellah peasants down there pumping up water from their wells in the same primitive way, using oxen and camels for power, driving their heavily laden donkeys, and generally tilling their fields with the same implements that had been used for generations back. They are industrious people but have intermittently been badly used by cruel pharaohs.

One cannot help but wonder what impression this country would have given the viewer centuries ago. Deep inside the desert petrified forests of enormous trees with thick trunks have been found buried under deep layers of sand. Once upon a time perhaps the great landowners from there hunted gazelles, lion, and other animals from their fast chariots, as depicted by the goldsmiths on the coffin found in the antechamber to Tutankhamen's last resting place.

It took us two hours to get to Mersa Matrûh. Last time I had been there we had landed on a dark night, as dark as a night can possibly be, with no stars or moon visible. That was now two years ago; I had been on my way from Europe in an old two-engined Dragon piloted by "Fatty" Pearson.*

---

*Alec "Fatty" Pearson was a very great friend of Blix's as well as mine. He was a terrific personality and outstanding pilot. He was a fighter pilot (Egypt and Crete) during the Second World War and later commanded the wing that supplied the 81st West African division in Burma. This division (in which I served) received all its supplies (weapons, ammunition, food, et cetera) from the air. While we were on leave together in Kashmir,

That aircraft was intended for safari transports to the remote coastal area between the Athi and Juba rivers and was well suited for this type of work, having low landing and takeoff speed requirements. We had arrived at Amseat somewhat behind schedule and were in a quandary about whether to carry on to Mersa Matrûh or stay overnight. Amseat was just a small village with a few huts and cottages, whereas Mersa Mathrûh had a good hotel, landing strip, and hangars.

We decided to continue and proceeded following the coastline. The weather was fine, the sun on its way down, and below us the foaming white breakers were visible. Fatty was humming a tune which apparently had something to do with a sailor's life and problems, the struts were singing, and the engines were droning away steadily. When the sun went down Fatty asked how much longer the daylight would last. "Thirty minutes." Five minutes later we passed a cliff on the coastline which I recognized from previous flights and knew that this landmark was exactly halfway between Mersa Maktrûh and Amseat. "What are we going to do?" asked the optimist, Fatty. "I would land on the road here below us and spend the night in the plane."—"Yes, that's very well, but it could be that you have miscalculated the distances—and in Mersa Matrûh we will have comfortable beds and a good dinner!" I gave advice, but he made the decisions. Another quarter of an hour and it was too dark to land on the road, which was no longer visible—we now had only the white line of the breakers to guide us. Fatty directed an electric torch towards the petrol gauge. Words were no longer necessary, and his fat fingers were drumming against the armrest of the pilot's seat. I smiled to myself; during the many years we had flown together, this was the first time I had seen my friend, the optimist, slightly perturbed. I tried to cheer him up by remarking that we could always land in the splash of the waves. "No comfortable bed there," was his curt reply.

Presently I saw a light—far, far away, but still a light.

"I can see Mersa Matrûh straight ahead!"

"I can't see any light."

"No, but I've seen it. Go up a bit."

And then we could clearly make out some blinking lights on the horizon. Lights always create hope; lights mean existence. Somebody must

---

he received the British and American DFCs and was recommended for the DSO. When we were on our way back to Burma, he was called to the UK, where he was killed shortly thereafter in a flying accident. G. F. V. K.

have lit them; somebody must be there. And so we winged in over Mersa
Matrûh, where we both had been previously. We knew the location of the
port and the direction of the railway line—but by then it was coal black.
We circled the town a few times, hoping that some intelligent individual
would be enterprising enough to take out one or two cars and with their
headlights give us an indication of the exact location of the landing strip.
We then dove repeatedly and made as much engine noise as possible, but
still no headlight could be seen. There was a completely dark area a
quarter of a mile from the harbor which we thought might be the airfield.
"I'm going to chance it!" said Fatty.

We made a perfect landing, the wheels were rolling, and the brakes
applied. We disembarked and, with the aid of a pocket torch, established
the fact that we had come to a standstill exactly five yards in front of the
hangar doors!

Eventually a car turned up, Customs and other formalities commenced—you know how good the Egyptian is at this sort of thing—and
it became too much for poor Fatty. The tension had been somewhat trying, so he parked his sixteen stone on the table, where he promptly fell
asleep. At last the formalities were over. We drove to the hotel, had a
bath, and drank a bottle of Pommery. Hell, that was then and is now past
history.

Now I was in Mersa Matrûh again, the white breakers curved against
the entrance to the port, and the Mediterranean glittered blue and invit-
ing. Beryl throttled down, the plane descended towards the ground,
straightened out, and a gentle landing was made. This time there would
be no beds and leisure. We had no time to spare and would have to hurry
with the clearing of documents, filling up with petrol, et cetera, as we
were going on to Amseat, across the border into Libya, and, if possible,
reaching Benghazi before night fell.

The Egyptian Customs officer recognized me. He was the very same
man who had become angry and suspicious when we landed in the dark
and Fatty had fallen asleep on his office table. This time, however, he was
courtesy personified. We had some grilled red mullet (one of the world's
best fishes) and a cup of strong coffee at the hotel, and by the time we had
finished the paperwork had been completed and the tanks filled. Just one
turn of the prop and the engine started, and once again our little bird
winged its way over Africa's desolate plains.

Amseat is the name of a small village, and this is where the politicians
have drawn up the boundary between Egypt and Libya and decided that

those living east of the line are Egyptians and those to the west Libyans. In order to be quite sure of this Mussolini has put up a wide barbed-wire fence along the demarcation line. What from the air looks like a blue ribbon stretching westwards from Amseat is really a tarmac road constructed like a European or American motorway.

We landed on the east side of the barbed wire, having circled over the rooftops of Sollum in order to alert the Customs official, who also kept the keys to the fuel store. The surface of the landing field was quite level but strewn with fist-sized stones which made the landing difficult for our small plane. The documents were soon cleared and we filled up with petrol ourselves. Then a turn of the prop, start, and a hop over the barbed wire and down again—in Libya, where the Italian flag fluttered over a white fort, Amseat. Here the runway was much better. Statues of Mussolini and Balbo were dimly visible at the end of a wide road. Some ten soldiers with fixed bayonets appeared and we produced our documents, whereupon an orderly disappeared with them. We took out the seat cushions and parked ourselves in the shadow of a wing. It was by then twelve o'clock and extremely hot. We sat there for two hours guarded like prisoners. At last the orderly returned with our papers (the whole procedure could easily have been completed in a couple of minutes), the police guard unfixed their bayonets, and we were allowed to leave Amseat. We received strict instructions on how to route our flight; it was forbidden to fly along the coast and over military encampments, and so we had to take a compass bearing over sand and desert.

As the great red globe of the sun was about to disappear behind the horizon we spotted the coast and Benghazi, and a few moments later we made our landing at the superb airport. We were met by friendly officials, and at the very good hotel we had a bottle of fresh, cool Chianti. No rooms, however, were available, as all accommodation was booked by the military. Finally, we found two rooms, spaghetti, good wine, and, best of all, a friendly reception from a kind old woman who kept a brothel.

Next morning there was a raging storm and the light sands of the desert rose like a black cloud over the town. The pepper trees were bent before the wind and the willow-like branches whipped about as if in a witches' dance. We motored out to the airport, where a meteorologist just then was busy measuring the wind force at higher altitudes with the aid of small colored balloons which he observed through a telescopic range finder. At three thousand feet he estimated the wind at twenty-five meters per second. Flying not possible, we were told, and we were not allowed to take off. The weather was too bad, and if we did not arrive at our destination within a reasonable amount of time, a search would have to be made.

Our luggage was already placed in the aircraft, the logbook was signed, and the tanks full. I looked at Beryl and said, "What do you think, do you really consider it necessary for us to spend another night here? The meteorologist maintains the storm will last for three days. Don't you think we should chance it?"—"The only thing I am perturbed about is the metal propeller," Beryl replied. "There is heavy gravel blowing all over the field, but if we can persuade them to let us fly, and to help by supporting the wings until the engine is warm, I am prepared to have a go!" I told the ground staff that the engine had coughed a bit when we had landed yesterday, would they assist us by holding onto the wings while Mrs. Markham revved the engine and I sat at the back of the cabin in order to keep the tail down?

Yes, this they were willing to do. The engine behaved as usual, three turns of the prop backwards and one forwards and it came alive. The Italians kindly held onto the wings, and after five minutes warming up I shouted at them, "Let go for a while and we'll see how she reacts!" Then Beryl accelerated and within twenty-five yards the strong headwind had us airborne. We swayed over bent date palms that were twisted, like human forms in agony, before the raging storm, and were carried skywards at terrific speed. The cloud of sand became lighter, the sun became visible, and under us we soon had a carpet of whirling dust. Beryl smiled and took out her compass bearing on Tripoli.

The airport at Tripoli is encircled by one of the world's best motor-racing tracks, and when I'd last been there and, like now, required petrol and Customs attendance, a Grand Prix race was in progress. That time we had landed at midday and wanted to continue our flight immediately, but alas the man who had had the keys to the petrol depot and the Customs personnel were all watching the race. With tempers rising, we had had to wait on the runway for six hours and eventually were forced to stay overnight, admittedly in the very comfortable Grand Hotel, but still not included in our flight plan. Remembering this, I asked Beryl to make a few turns around the track to see if there was a race in progress. However, everything was quiet, the track was empty and deserted, and we taxied smoothly up to the Shell petrol pumps. Our documents were inspected and signed in the usual manner, and after a light lunch we continued on to Tunis.

When on a flight to Europe, as we were now, there is something very special about Tunis. It means farewell to Africa; after that there is just the long hop over the Mediterranean. It means good-bye to the palm trees, and to the free and easy life. You fly straight into a different existence, with all its rules and regulations, formal manners, black and white tie, et cetera.

Tunis is a pretty town with palms, plane trees, and poinsettias. Imposing avenues are lined with white houses, and colorful buses and trams are interspersed with gleaming luxury cars and distinguished conveyances of all sorts. Fiery Arab horses with flying manes trot ever so lightly in front of elegant carriages. Out there we have the glorious Mediterranean, always beautiful and sparkling, and above us the sky forms an almost permanently deep blue vault.

After a few minutes' argument with the hall porter we managed to each get a room with a bath. It was early summer. The fruit trees were in full blossom, the lawns were as green as could be, the birds were singing and flitting around their nests, guitars were being strummed, and one could hear accordion music and song from every alley.

Early next morning we were at the airport and waved good-bye to Africa in glorious sunshine. The engine was singing and buzzing—our little bluebird was on its way home. Cagliari could be glimpsed a few degrees to the west and we were soon over Bizerte. Down below was the town, looking like another Deauville, with the turquoise sea breaking in a foaming surf. Here and there the wakes from boats were etched as fine silver lines on the infinite blue surface and the smoke from their funnels floated like veils in the clear air.

The route we were given was extremely complicated. We were not allowed to approach Cagliari from the sea but had to follow the eastern coastline and then head inland through a corridor until we reached the town from the north—the kitchen entrance so to speak. Neither Beryl nor I knew anything about military fortifications, but this fact we could not expect the authorities to know. Beryl navigated and put the plane down as softly as if she was handling a baby. It was a military landing strip and uniformed personnel approached at great speed. With much flag waving we steered in between rows of enormous hangars. A senior officer arrived in a car—our British markings had been noticed. "How do you do? Welcome," et cetera. "We just want to have the tanks filled before leaving for Nice."—"Yes, but it is already three o'clock and the weather report is unfavorable."—"Oh, we'll get there in time if we can only buy our aviation spirits straight away."—"No, it's too risky; you'll have to wait for better weather. I will, however, book rooms for you at the hotel and get you a car." So this time, Beryl's fair curls and blue eyes had no effect.

The car arrived and we drove to the hotel with one policeman on each running board and an air force officer next to the driver. Suspicious officers imagined that we might be spies and rumors of this had already reached town, where a crowd of hundreds of people had gathered in front of the hotel. Again we had trouble with the hall porter because we did not want to share rooms.

We had our meal in our rooms, in bad humor—spaghetti and Chianti.

Not till three o'clock the following day did we get our tanks filled and were allowed to leave, in miserable weather. It was entirely due to Beryl's skill as a pilot that we even got to France.

And so now we are back in Europe again. Many friends met us here, mail, telephone messages, and telegrams were waiting for us, and it was wonderful to taste French food and champagne. I tried to phone you from Nice but was unable to get hold of you.

It was a bit more difficult than usual to wake up the following morning, but up I got. It really is a beautiful trip from this Mediterranean town with the Swiss Alps to the north. We fly over smiling valleys watered by foaming streams, and the slopes are dotted with picturesque cottages. High above, the perpetual snow glitters on the mountaintops and the rays of sun perform a blinding dance on the bright glacier slopes.

While our documents were checked and the plane was being refueled we had a quick lunch at the Lyon airport restaurant. And so—Paris. I had sent a quick wire to Frank* at the Ritz bar asking him to inform Sosthenes de la Rochefoucauld (if he was in town) that I was on my way, and Beryl had arranged a meeting with some duchess.

Things, however, do not always turn out as planned. Time passed and where was Paris? The deviation had been greater than calculated by Beryl, and we passed the capital to the east, flew over the Marne, and followed the river back again. As it was getting dark, we approached the town at low altitude, in spite of regulations. Now we could discern the Eiffel Tower against the horizon and a little later we landed at Le Bourget. We taxied past the deserted hangars till we reached one that Beryl recognized. A surly old man who was in a hurry to get home opened the sliding doors. *Voila!* and we pushed in the plane.

"Customs?"

---

*Barman at the Ritz.

"*Non, non, monsieur,* it is too late for that!"

I put my suitcase in a shed, only taking what I needed for the night. There was another man in the shed fiddling with his luggage and as he was leaving I thought I recognized his gait—however, it could not very well be *that* person because he was in Spain. Yet who else walked in that particular way, with those long arms like a gorilla's?

"Ernest!" I shouted, and sure enough, it was Ernest Hemingway, unshaven and dirty, but him, without a doubt.

"What are you doing here?"

"I could ask the same." I from Africa and he from the Spanish Civil War.

We drove together to the Ritz, both unwashed and him with a week's growth of beard. Behind the bar was George instead of Frank, and he fixed us up with rooms, dinner, telephone calls, mail—everything.

"But, Ernest, what are you doing here?"

"I have just come from the Spanish Frontier. Why don't you go there and shoot humans instead of lions!"

But I know Ernest. He no more wanted to kill humans than I liked to shoot lions, but he wanted to know why and how it was done, and how a few individuals could cause tens of thousands to behave like animals (this is wrongly put and doing animals an injustice). He wanted to know how to put the brakes on the fanaticism of the human race. It is so much easier to fan the flames of hate and annoyance than to dampen and extinguish them again. You also know Ernest, so there is no need for me to tell you this, but I took it as a good omen meeting him just after our landing.

Sosthenes was the same as always, and we sat up and talked all night. Next day we had to enjoy the chestnuts in blossom, so we've only arrived in London today, and tomorrow *we* will meet. Therefore there was really no need for me to write this letter.

With all my love,
Blix

FURTHER READING

Readers wanting to learn more about the life and times of Bror Blixen might like to read the following books:

Aschan, Ulf. *The Man Whom Women Loved: The Life of Bror Blixen.* St. Martin's Press, 1987.

Baker, Carlos. *Ernest Hemingway: A Life Story.* Avon Books, 1980.

Chalmers, Patrick R. *Sport and Travel in East Africa: Compiled from the Private Diaries of HRH the Prince of Wales.* Philip Alan, 1934.

Dinesen, Isak (Karen Blixen). *Out of Africa* and *Shadows on the Grass.* Random House, 1985.

————. *Letters from Africa.* University of Chicago Press, 1984.

Holman, Dennis. *Inside Safari Hunting.* W.H. Allen, 1969.

Huxley, Elspeth. *Out in the Midday Sun.* Viking Books, 1987.

Lovell, Mary S. *Straight On Till Morning: The Authorized Biography of Beryl Markham.* St. Martin's Press, 1987.

Markham, Beryl. *West with the Night.* North Point Press, 1983.

Thurman, Judith. *Isak Dinesen: The Life of a Storyteller.* St. Martin's Press, 1982.

Von Blixen-Finecke, Baron Bror. *African Hunter.* St. Martin's Press, 1986.